MATERIAL CULTURE
AND TEXT

MATERIAL CULTURES
Interdisciplinary studies in the material construction of social worlds

Series editors: Daniel Miller, *Department of Anthropology, University College London;* Michael Rowlands, *Department of Anthropology, University College London;* Christopher Tilley, *Department of Archaeology, St David's University College, Wales.*

The Material Cultures series crosses the traditional subject boundaries of archaeology, history and anthropology to consider human society in terms of its production, consumption and social structures. This approach breaks down the narrow compartmentalization which has until now obscured understanding of past and present societies and offers a more broadly-based (and coherent) set of explanations.

The series has developed from frustration with the conceptual limits imposed by a structure of separate disciplines. These divisions make little sense when so much of the most valuable work in many areas – in archaeology, consumption studies, architecture, museology, human geography, anthropology and communication science – grows from common roots and a shared intellectual framework.

The thrust of the series is to develop concepts necessary for understanding cultural and social form; but the editors' approach reverses the primacy often given to linguistic over material structures. This is deliberate after all, although structuralism borrowed from linguistics it took its most original shape through Lévi-Strauss's studies of kinship, myth and ritual. More recently a parrallel process has taken place in architecture, which has been a crucial focus in the development of theories of post-modernism. This suggests that there are many advantages in attempting to construct approaches to the material world which consciously proclaim the distinctive nature of *objects* as against *language*.

This approach, central to all the books in the series, should be of particular benefit to those studies (like archaeology) which have artefacts as their main focus. But materiality provides new perceptions of cultural context over a much wider range of subject matter.

It demands a conscious process of linking together the techniques and strategies of other disciplines. For example, a recognition of the issues of gender will infuse an historically based study with a deeper set of meanings; set the same work within an anthropological framework as well, and its value (and insights) are enhanced.

This broad sense of context allows us to publish work on the cultural politics of the body, on power systems of representation, on food and gender, and the experience of possession or alienation. All of them are rooted within a materialist interpretation of culture.

The series will maintain a productive dialogue with developments in Marxist, as well as structuralist, post-structuralist and phenomenological thought, through focusing on the *specificity* of the material world and its particular forms and contents. Yet we recognize that it is the very materiality of that world which often presents a challenge to theory and promotes a critical approach to analysis.

Many of the disciplines which have a particular concern with material culture, such as museology and consumption studies, have tended to feel that their own developments in theory and analysis have been neglected over previous decades. They have become, relatively speaking, backwaters of the social science. This series is launched at a time when there are signs that this is about to be radically changed.

There are new advances in cultural theory which are not merely fetishistic and do not posit the object as distinct from social and cultural context. Advances in post-structuralism which have challenged the notion of the subject mean that we are now free to conceive of a new approach to material culture, which does not privilege or reify either objects or persons.

In planning and co-ordinating the series we wish to demonstrate above all the current intellectual excitement and potential for working within this field. Creating meaning from the material fragments of the past and the present now provides an arena for addressing some of the fundamental theoretical and philosophical issues of our time.

MATERIAL CULTURE AND TEXT

The Art of Ambiguity

CHRISTOPHER TILLEY

ROUTLEDGE

London and New York

First published in 1991
by Routledge
11 New Fetter Lane, London EC4P 4EE
Simultaneously published in the USA and Canada by Routledge
a division of Routledge, Chapman and Hall Inc.
29 West 35th Street, New York, NY 10001

© 1991 Christopher Tilley

Typeset by J&L Composition Ltd, Filey, North Yorkshire
Printed in Great Britain by T. J. Press, Padstow, Cornwall

British Library Cataloguing in Publication Data
Tilley, Christopher
Material culture and text: the art of ambiguity. –
(Material cultures).
1. Archaeology. Theories
I. Title   II. Series
930.101

Library of Congress Cataloging in Publication Data
Tilley, Christopher Y.
Material culture and text: the art of ambiguity/
Christopher Tilley.
p.   cm.
Includes bibliographical references and index.
1. Archaeology–Methodology. 2. Material culture. I. Title.
CC75.7.T55 1991
930.1′028–dc20   90–36313
ISBN 0 415 05588 1

CONTENTS

CONTENTS

ILLUSTRATIONS

TABLES

PREFACE

This book was written in two periods, between October 1987 and February 1988 and March to September 1989. Early versions of parts of the manuscript were presented in Copenhagen, Göteborg and Oslo and later ones in London. I am grateful for the critical comments I received on these occasions. I would like to thank a number of friends and colleagues who have directly or indirectly been responsible for the completion of this book: Barbara Bender, Grant Chambers, Ian Hodder, Danny Miller, Bjørn Myhre, Jarl Nordbladh, Bjørnar Olsen, Mike Rowlands, Mike Shanks and Stig Welinder. Barbara Bender and Bjørnar Olsen were kind enough to constructively criticize parts of the text. A few paragraphs in this book have appeared in print elsewhere.

Part I

READING A MATERIAL TEXT

Figure 1 View of the rapids and islands at Nämforsen downriver, taken from the north-east, with the Island of Brådön in the centre, 1939 (After Hallström 1960: Photo 63)

Figure 2 Brådön viewed from Notön at high water 1907 (After Hallström 1960: Photo 113)

1
MOTIFS AND RAPIDS

Figure 3 View of the rapids (Photo: Gösta Westman)

Nämforsen. In the late spring, the roar of the water can be heard from a considerable distance. The tree-clad cliffs forming the northern river banks rise here to a height of more than 60 m providing a panoramic view. In the midst of an expanse of towering pine forest the turbulent water crashes over the rocks and whirls in a series of magnificent rapids, between 3000 and 2000 BC the last barrier before a long narrow inlet of the open sea. On bare, glossy rock surfaces polished by ice and water, along the margins of the river shores, and on two islands in the river course surrounded by the seething water, is an enormous accumulation of carved or pecked motifs.

Some images which fascinate me:

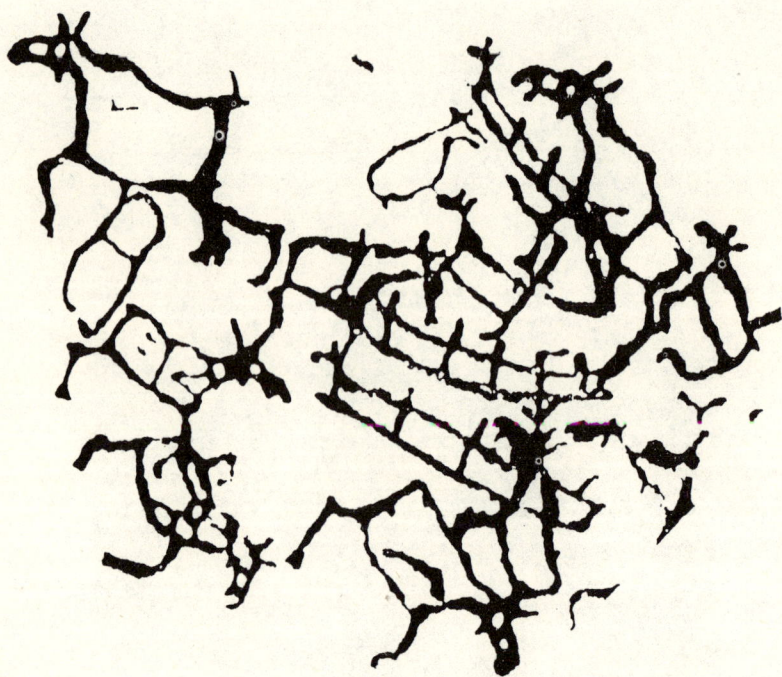

Figure 4 A writhing mass of elks interspersed with boats and shoe sole

Figure 5   A 'love scene' overlooked by an elk

Figure 6   Phallic man and double-headed elk

5

Figure 7 A couple, one figure with marked swelling in the belly, stand by an upturned elk head

Figure 8 Boats transform into elks

Figure 9 Elks transform into humans

Figure 10 What is it?

Time and humanity have altered and transformed these traces of the past: transported blocks of ice or stone abrade, rocks crack and split, their surfaces transfigured. Black lichen and other vegetation grow in areas no longer exposed to the full force of the waters; fires made by fishermen against the cold; rock blasting to aid the salmon catch or log floating; the construction of timber ballast beds and a hydroelectric power plant – all these have combined to obscure the physical remnants of the past.

But time has also added to original event and experience: a textual accretion continues to grow. The carved rock surfaces are now overlain by an opaque slime sticky with words and figurational representations. Nämforsen has been disseminated and may now be 'seen' not only in Ångermanland, northern Sweden, but in Stockholm, London, New York or Rio de Janeiro. Already an interpretation of an interpretation, the carvings provide an infinitely expansive medium of discourse – at times frothy with the agitation of reaching absent meaning – which simultaneously reveals and obscures.

Their failure to disclose social signification has resulted in the deadening verbal and visual catalogue of the empiricist archaeological text, the 'standard' work from which subsequent chronological and chorological obsessions take their point of departure, attempting to pin the carvings down as precisely as possible in space and time. But of social and cultural and cosmological context so little has been said.

What is to be made of these rock carvings? Since they are so

7

utterly removed from contemporary experience, must our reaction to them always remain one of alienation? What is their meaning, significance and value today? Our reaction may be one of fascination but must this inevitably be reflected in interpretative incompetence, a dumb failure to discover meaning? Or can we hope to mediate them productively, reinscribe them into the present, open out the carvings to subjective experience once more?

2

NÄMFORSEN THROUGH THE EYES OF HALLSTRÖM

Hallström devoted most of his active working life – forty years – to documenting the rock carvings of northern Norway and Sweden, producing two massive catalogues of the finds with appended dossiers of plates (1938, 1960). His work on Nämforsen, documented in *Monumental Art of Northern Sweden from the Stone Age* and published only two years before his death, in many respects marks the culminating point of his work. Nämforsen, only partially documented previously, was, after Hallström, the largest known conglomeration of rock carvings in the whole of Europe, only exceeded by Val Camonica in northern Italy (and now, more recently, Alta in arctic Norway). In the face of the ravages associated with the construction of a hydroelectric plant 'absolutely special means and measures, beyond those usually available to scientific research and the care of ancient monuments' were required (Hallström 1960: x).

The title of Hallström's book appears odd, the average size of the rock carvings being about 40 cm. He himself remarks on this in the preface (p. ix) and initially suggests it was an attempt to find an adequate expression to convey a sense of the sheer quantities of the carvings. In the conclusion we have another clue: Hallström notes that this is a 'heavy book' (p. 370). He in fact transforms a disparate series of documents (individual rock carving surfaces) into a monument. That which is truly monumental is Hallström's effort – the book itself, the long years of dedication, the supreme effort of will to complete it in his later years, despite failing health. Mobilized and compressed into a bound text, the rock carvings serve as Hallström's personal monument, his claim to immortality. This monument, although signed under the aegis of a proper name, is paradoxically more like a gravestone without any inscription, for it signifies a

9

textual space that is meant to exclude its author: an object intended to be unmediated by a constitutive subjectivity.

Hallström's aim was to present a scientific treatise, to document the rock carvings for posterity with the greatest possible rigour, omitting no detail. Such 'scientific' treatment meant (and still means) that any interpretative understanding of the rock carvings had to be reduced or confined to an absolute minimum. Beyond the descriptive catalogue and the plates detailing what and where, the less said the better, for this would be to stray beyond the permitted bounds of discourse. Of the 205 pages of the text Hallström devotes to Nämforsen, 141 or 69 per cent consists of a description of different rock carving surfaces. A further fifty pages simply enumerate, compare and contrast the different categories of carvings – human figures, boats, birds, etc. delineated in the main catalogue.

Hallström's research at Nämforsen was carried out primarily between 1934 and 1947, supplemented by work on smaller sites, and there can be no doubt about his dedication to the task. He notes almost drowning in the rapids on one occasion with his wife, building bridges out to isolated rocks in the seething river channel, crawling with smarting hands over precipitous and rough rock surfaces, searching the area by day and by night with floodlights and in any and every possible type of weather, checking out accounts of local people and previous antiquaries who had been to the site. Few stones indeed were left either unturned or untrodden. Such determination can only be admired and the finished catalogue is an exemplary piece of documentation executed to the highest possible standards, for which we all owe him a great debt.

The interpretative result: 'this concluding chapter obviously does not present any conclusion' (1960: 377). Hallström's entire life's work ends without any conclusion. In this sense it is a complete failure. He clearly has little more grasp of the meaning and significance of the rock carvings at the end than he had at the beginning. All he can finally say, a few lines before the book ends, is that 'the most important thing is the material' (p. 377). But this failure was built into Hallström's project from the very beginning, predetermined. He cannot conclude, cannot say anything about the meaning or significance of the carvings, because the premises (largely unexamined) from which he worked systematically prevented him from doing so.

He states that the task of the student of rock carvings is twofold: to document them as precisely as possible and interpret them 'in the best possible way' (p. xiv), a position which appears to be reasonable enough but actually contains the seeds of its own dissolution. It becomes increasingly clear in Hallström's text that to document as 'precisely as possible' systematically blocks not only the 'best possible' interpretation but any interpretation at all. What does Hallström mean by this term 'interpretation'? He never cares to specify what this concept is supposed to imply or involve. He writes of 'mastering' the carvings, a 'need for a penetration into the essence of this rock-art' (p. 366), of 'reading' the figures, and at one point even employs a military metaphor – he wants to 'conquer' them (p. 138). This mastering, conquering, penetration and reading of what he speculates might be considered to be 'the literature of the period' (p. 370) involves repeated checking of figures on different rock surfaces, at different times, in different seasons, in different lighting conditions, during the day and at night. This may permit eventually, and given luck and circumstance, the reading of the 'literature', the carved rock surfaces.

Hallström 'reads' in a rather peculiar way: words without subjects or objects, without referents, without sentences, lacking any structure, any grammatical system. Hallström's is a reading which can never recover meaning. 'The cat sat on the mat' or 'mat the on sat cat the' or 'the mat the sat on cat' all 'mean' the same thing to him – all are equally meaningless word combinations because what he designates as important is not relationships between words but the words themselves. So in any sentence Hallström does not differentiate between nouns or verbs or adjectives and has no understanding of signifiers and signifieds or phonemes. 'Cat' and 'on' etc. are recognized as singular units but are ascribed exactly the same significance or importance. Where they appear in relation to each other does not matter. Of course, Hallström has a problem: he is not reading his own language but one some 4,000 years old and there are many gaps in the text. But if we insist on reading words on a page with no sense of any real relationships between them, we are left with a meaningless pattern and as Hallstrom reads rock carvings in this way he simply cannot understand them.

In essence, for Hallström to read or to interpret the rock carvings is to identify. Interpretation becomes a process of identification; the two terms are thoroughly conflated. So, once it has been decided that a group of carved lines can be identified as an animal rather than a fish it has been interpreted. Where conditions permit, such an interpretation may be more fully fleshed out by, for example, specifying species or determining numbers of legs or fins. Such identification virtually (but not entirely – see below) exhausts meaning. An elk is an elk is an elk and ... so what?

Hallström uses the terms 'subjective' and 'objective' fairly frequently and, of course, he wants to be as objective as possible. This is what he attempts to do by the wearing and ceaseless process of identification, although even this operation is flawed with ambiguities and uncertainties. Comments such as: 'the carving is difficult to read on account of wear. I have obtained different detailed readings every time' (p. 195) repeatedly intersperse his text. Hallström is denied even the solace of total objectivity which, like interpretation, is ultimately only another name for identification.

Hallström is a pure empiricist subscribing to a rigid doctrine of atomistic particularism in which it is assumed that nothing is related unless it can be proved otherwise so the occurrence of the same or different figures on the same or different rock surfaces has no necessary significance. The only possible proof of any relationship is ascribed to the realm of sense perception: individual rock carvings are not related unless joined in some way, unless there is a visible connection. But even here the question arises as to whether such a fusion of figures is intentional or mere coincidence (see e.g. p. 221 or p. 308).

For Hallström an eruptive immediacy gives the rock carvings their form and character. To interpret their significance requires no more than a single jump from perception to judgement: an elk *means* an elk. The observer's impression of form becomes an actual category of subsequent contemplation and, since this contemplation is always to be tied down and grounded in the realistic, the process of understanding automatically ends. Even the most disconcerting and striking of the juxtapositions of various motif categories on individual rock surfaces are explained away as a logical result of a gradual accumulation of depictions. Hallström's thought remains always rooted in the particular and the apodictic. The carvings are understood as individual products of prehistoric artisans rather than as a social production transcending individual agency. There is no 'denying that there is a distinct thought behind every figure executed on the rock' (p. 366), although such particular thoughts linked to particular carvings are now, of course, irrevocably lost.

Although identification virtually exhausts meaning, or at least that which may be communicated by the analyst, a little more may be stated. It may perhaps be possible to situate the rock carvings, on a comparative basis, in time and space. Are the carvings at Nämforsen older or younger than those in Norway or southern Sweden or Russia and where did the ideas or influences come from? Hallström's choice of the most immediately recognizable form determines his understanding of the significance of the creation and reception of the carvings. Their form is regarded as necessary. Nämforsen is considered to be a relatively late stage in the evolution of the totality of northern Scandinavian rock carvings (p. 369). Within this evolutionary process the styles (from carved outline figures to silhouette forms entirely scooped out of the rock surface) become organic developments, rooted in changing ways of depicting reality. Discussing the stylistic form of a particular category of rock carvings Hallström states that 'a connection (Reindeer Island [Russia] – Lehtojärvi [Finland] – Nämforsen or vice versa) can hardly be doubted' (p. 317). So a connection between rock carvings more than 800 km distant (as the empiricist walks – or in this case must also swim – across the Gulf of Bothnia) is possible while one involving distances of 5 or 10 cm is ruled out of court. Although, when stated in this manner, this may appear somewhat odd, it is entirely consistent. The carvings at Nämforsen and in Russia are again linked by a process of identification: they look the same so there must be a connection. Animals and boats, by contrast, do not share the same visible features, so when appearing on the same rock surface, even if separated by only a few centimetres, or if actually conjoined, no meaningful relationship may be countenanced.

Hallström finds the word 'cat' in Swedish and Russian but he has no conceptual apparatus to translate these languages. Moreover, he can only speculate as to how they could possibly be connected: movement of 'guilds' of craftsmen, or ideas or influences or religions or trade. The list goes on until eventually we find ourselves back with the material again – now with appended identifications. This is all that ultimately matters about the past – its materiality, its identification, the monotony of the same ... and here was another elk.

Hallström's relation to Nämforsen, like that of any excavator to his or her site, is a privileged one. No one is likely in the foreseeable future to possess such detailed empirical experience of it – the very publication of his book and plates in fact militates against this, as does the gradual physical erosion of the site. We can be sure that the meanings of the carvings must have been constantly on his mind: 'during the long lifetime that I have devoted to the problems of the rock art ... I have imagined that I realized more and more clearly the forces that formed and transformed the spiritual habitus of the territory' (p. 370) yet these thoughts remained bottled up, presumably considered unacceptable for public presentation. There is a clear separation between Hallström the man and Hallström the archaeologist, between private and public knowledge. Hallström cuts a figure of pathos, a man who could perhaps say so much but in fact says so little.

The only information deemed suitable for public dissemination involves questions of quantity, distribution, identity and chronology. To expose his private 'imaginings' would be to transgress one of the unwritten rules of archaeological discourse and invade a public space of communal and sacred archaeological knowledge. That which is sacred must be empirically verifiable, tied down, grounded in immediate experience of the object. But the detachment of Hallström's subjectivity simultaneously results in an embargo on finding meaning in the carvings. Hallström follows an empiricist philosophy through in a particularly rigid manner to its logical conclusion – silence. Yet he is hardly alone in adopting this philosophical position. Archaeology is, and has always been, dominated by varieties of empiricism and the question of social meaning and significance of material representations seriously abbreviated as a consequence. Meaning is not seen: it is a production.

Pathos, tragedy, alienation, the loss of subjective meaning – most would feel this but Hallström would not. He, no doubt, had more of the instinct of the typically Victorian collector. He was not interested in argument or discussion but documentation, the compilation of an immense inventory of facts, a bureaucratic archive, an insatiable hunger for more material, a never ending quest to reveal the totality of the evidence. In this labour of documentation Hallström had the passionate intensity and conscientiousness of a man who knew himself to be a custodian of treasures. But what are we to do with them? Decorate the museum?

I have, of course, been deliberately provocative and unfair to Hallström. I am immensely grateful to his effort and this book is parasitic on his. He has been deliberately decontextualized. Most academic books up to the 1960s had minimal conclusions. The point of most texts was to provide material, which was largely an end in itself. His work cannot then be described as a failure in its own period or times. Hallström's unsuspecting role in this text has been to provide a particularly vivid example of an attitude of mind, a genre of academic writing, both pervasive in much research on Scandinavian rock carvings, and indeed in contemporary archaeology as a whole. Our concern here goes entirely beyond Hallström as agent. He exemplifies the tragedy of much contemporary archaeology – painstaking, almost masochistic effort, an immense labour, but a failure to disclose meaning. What this amounts to is an evasion of the responsibility to make sense of the past. This evasion stems from fear – fear of the implications stemming from the vital significance of the subjective experience of the archaeologist.

The importance of the subjective is not to be taken here in any simple sense. The position being advocated is not one implying a rampant and untrammelled subjectivism with each archaeologist locked into and creating his or her own past: in the case in hand, grafting his or her personalized consciousness onto the rock carvings to create unique sets of incommensurable meanings. Subjective experience is important only in so far as there is a genuine dialectic of subjectivity and objectivity, the modification of the one by the other, in the process of reaching understanding. Furthermore the subjective is not to be conceived as the personal, ultimately the narcissistic, but in terms of itself being an objective construct, i.e. the modified consciousness of a social being. I can speak of 'myself' without the 'my' being taken as simply constituting 'the self'. 'My' subjectivity is the result of a process of a *bricolage* of ideas, influences, readings, lectures, activities commencing at birth. 'My' self is an entity shot through with the traces of others.

3

LOCATING A GRAMMAR

MATERIAL CULTURE, WRITING

In virtually all discussions of the social, language is held to be the primary distinguishing feature of humanity. All socialized persons speak or communicate with each other. In a process of dialogue this communication between persons is both direct and transient. Language flows but is not materially fixed or sedimented. Fixation and sedimentation occur in the process of writing. We know empirically that writing, in the sense of a phonetic script, is a relatively late development, something that is secondary, derivative and attempts to mimic speech through the production of graphic marks on a page. For any writing to be intelligible, for us to be able to read it and hear the sounds in our head, there must be a textual practice of spacing and differentiation. To put this simply, we must at least be able to recognize where one word ends, the next begins, and be able to distinguish differences between words. However, as Derrida cogently states (Derrida 1976), practices involving spacing, differentiation, articulation and rearticulation of units or entities form a primordial part of human consciousness. In this sense writing in the special sense of an *archewriting* precedes the spoken word. Speech, then, is derivative from an originary material 'writing' dialectically related to human activity in the world. Phonetic scripts are only a particular type of writing, a derivative and secondary logocentric manner of conveying speech. The important point to be made here is that speech, phonetic writing and material culture all involve a similar materialist practice: they are all transformations of a primordial human practice, variations on the same theme, sharing common qualities. All are fundamentally to do with communication between persons and the creation of meaning. Material culture is 'written' through a practice of spacing and differentiation in just the same manner as phonetic writing. Both result in the material fixation of meaning which, by contrast to speech, is indirectly communicated in the sense that I decorate a pot by dividing up the empty space of the clay or write a letter by inscribing marks on a blank sheet of paper and at some time in the future you read and interpret the visual medium, able by virtue of the material fixation to read what I have produced.

So far I have made the basic point that material culture, speech and writing all share the same qualities but that communication through speech is more direct. They involve different transformations of the same materialist practice of spacing, differentiation, articulation. In other words all these practices are structured in precisely the same way through breaking up space (or silence in the case of the spoken word), creating and establishing difference, articulating and rearticulating units. However, as everyone knows, to make even the simplest statement such as 'It is raining' with material objects would be rather difficult. In fact it would be a complete waste of time and effort. Material culture does not communicate meaning content in the same way as speech or the phonetic script – that would constitute needless duplication. It rather makes different types of communicative statements but structured in a way that may be, in part, analogous. The meaning content of these material culture statements cannot be decided or specified in an *a priori* way in theory, just as we cannot decide in advance what a book will say if we have not read it. Hence in this section I am not concerned with the specific meaning content of material culture but rather with the question of how meaning comes into being in a material culture text.

LANGUAGE AND SPEECH
IN MATERIAL CULTURE

In his *Course in General Linguistics* [1916] (1966) Saussure introduces a crucial distinction between language and speech. A language (*langue*) is something collectively shared, a social institution with a systemic quality, a set of norms shared and participated in by individuals who can neither create nor modify it by themselves. Language is like a game with rules and in order to play the game (speak and be comprehended) individuals have to abide by these rules. Speech (*parole*) is an individual act in which the codes provided by language are utilized to express something. Speech is essentially combinatory in nature, articulating elements of *langue*. Language and speech are dialectically related; neither can exist without the other. Language provides the conditions or underlying structure for any speech act or writing to take place while, without speech acts, language would no longer exist. Any act of speaking or writing is a concrete material phenomenon. It can be heard or seen. Language, by contrast, has no concrete existence in an act of speech. It exists in a community of speakers generally at an unconscious level: we can speak while having no knowledge of the language that permits us to do so. *Langue* is not reducible to the individuals who make up that community. It provides a medium for speech and is at the same time reproduced or transformed through speech acts: a medium and outcome of speech in the world. Phonetic writing is a formalization of speech by individuals who all interpret it in the same way. We might say, in a highly abstract manner, that writing comes between *langue* and *parole,* corresponding to what Hjelmslev referred to as usage. When thinking about usage we are concerned with actual linguistic practices existing in a society at any one time, intimately bound up with social context, with power, institutions and particular groups. We leave in the background a notion of *langue* to which each individual speaker bears a similar and generalized relation and instead consider discursive formations and their relation to strategies of dominance and resistance (see pp. 153–5).

The terms 'language' and 'speech', although by no means ideal, can readily be used to understand non-verbal communicative practices in general and material culture in particular. Barthes (1984) gives examples of garment systems, food systems and furniture systems looked at from this perspective. The 'language' in the garment system is made up by (i) oppositions of pieces of garment (trousers, shirt, hat, etc.), variations in which entail a change in meaning (bowler hats do not mean the same thing as cloth caps); (ii) rules by which items of clothing are associated on the body or in layers. 'Speech' in the garment system would involve different details of individual fabrication or manner of wearing the clothes: free association of pieces, degree of cleanliness (Barthes 1984: 93–4).

In the food system we can differentiate between an 'alimentary language' made up of rules of exclusion (alimentary taboos), opposition of units (e.g. savoury/sweet), simultaneous levels of association at the level of the dish (sausages and potatoes rather than sausages and custard), temporal levels of association (fish course, meat course, sweet course). 'Alimentary speech' consists of all the personal or family variations of food preparation and association. This can also be considered at the level of the menu:

> Any menu is concocted with reference to a structure (which is both national – or regional – and social); but this structure is filled differently according to the days and users, just as linguistic 'form' is filled by the free variations and combinations which a speaker needs for a particular message. The relationship between language and speech would here be fairly similar to that which is found in verbal language: broadly, it is usage, that is to say, a sort of sedimentation of many people's speech, which makes up the alimentary language; however, phenomena of individual variation can acquire an institutional value within it.
>
> (Barthes 1984: 94–5)

Douglas (1975) has elaborated on this basic theme. As part of the alimentary language we can distinguish between 'heavy' and 'light' dishes, meals and snacks, meals appropriate at certain times of the day (breakfast, lunch, dinner and the foods appropriate for each), between solids and liquids, socially valued primary and secondary components (meat and vegetables) and so on. The social valuation of foodstuffs is an important component of *langue*: you are what you eat; you are also whom you eat with and where and how.

As these examples show the *langue/parole* distinction can readily be extended to non-verbal practices in a general way. Other examples, drawn from material culture studies, are readily available. We can speak of a 'language of pot design' by which we refer to (i) rules of graphic practice – what can and cannot occur; (ii) rules of combinations of designs (e.g. whether a triangle can occur only below a circle in the rim area of a pot); (iii) rules of contextual association between various pot types and houses, graves, etc. The 'speech of pot design' would be variation in the execution and types of designs on any particular pot. The 'language of grave goods' includes what is or is not appropriate to place in a grave and where (by the head, feet, etc.) and according to other features such as age, sex, status, etc. The 'speech' would be individual variations on this basic *langue*. But material culture is not, of course, 'spoken' but 'written': materially inscribed. If we now shift over to thinking about how we might read material culture 'writing', we realize that, like reading a phonetic script, it is necessary to isolate the elements or words of which it is composed. This is readily apparent through the practice of spacing in their material inscription. It has already been noted that this is a practice extending to, or rather from, material culture. The recognition of units and boundaries between the elements is usually readily apparent: individual pots, graves, houses, dishes composing a meal, items of clothing. We can also consider all these things in terms of an hierarchical structure: a pot with individual designs on it, a house with items of furniture arranged in it, a grave with grave goods, and so on. Depending on the level of our analysis we will identify different words or meaning units and can consider their articulation in terms of the sentences in which they appear to create a text. For example, a design on a pot can be considered as formally equivalent to a word, and its components as phonemes. Different designs on the same pot serve to articulate a sentence. A set of pots in a house or a settlement can be conceived as a text situated in relation to other texts. Material culture patterning characteristically consists of sentences and texts within texts. For example, a series of pots in a grave may form a sentence constituting part of the text of a cemetery. In other words the text of material culture is like an edited book, sentences written by different authors within a text constituting a larger overall text.

SIGNIFICATION

Speech and writing signify – they communicate meaning and in an analogous way material culture constitutes a significative structure of meanings. In other words objects do not just 'mean' themselves. A pot is not just a pot and an axe is not just an axe, a design on a pot is not just marks on clay. We can regard all individual items of material culture as *signs* in some ways equivalent to linguistic signs (other terms sometimes substituted for 'sign' include signal, icon, symbol). Saussure proposed that the linguistic sign involved a diacritical relation between a signifier and a signified, which together form a union in the sign. The sign, then, is like a coin with two sides which are inseparable from each other. The signifier is an audible sound referring to a particular concept or thing, the signified. The relationship between the two remains arbitrary, a matter of historical and social convention. A signified is not a thing but a mental representation of it; the signified of the word 'horse' is therefore not the four-legged animal but a mental representation of it. The sign only gains meaning diacritically from the overall system of *langue* in which horse is only horse because it is not cow, rat or dog and vice versa. Thus meaning inheres in *difference* and is always relational. Signs in isolation could not exist, because they would have no meaning. It does not matter how a signifier appears so long as it preserves its difference from others. Signification is a process binding together the signifier and the signified and it is important to note that the linguistic sign may be arbitrary in an *a priori* sense (in English we use 'dog', in French 'chien') to refer to the same mental representation of an animal, but it is not in an *a posteriori* sense. Once it has been grounded in tradition it becomes naturalized, appears as obvious. In other words, signs are grounded in tradition which affects their usage, which is always social.

All this has important implications in terms of a semiological translation from the linguistic sign to a non-linguistic or non-verbal sign. We can classify these material signs into various types, e.g. gestural, iconic, graphic, and in terms of their relations to functional items: pots, houses, axes, etc. Once a set of material culture signs has been established through their difference, their relationship is likely to remain relatively non-arbitrary through time. We can expect structured repetition to preserve a relation of difference. In order to analyse the meaning of these signs we need to pay attention to their contextual relationships (e.g. does a pot of type *x* with design *a* always appear in the grave of a woman?) and the differences between them. We will be focusing on qualities rather than quantities. In other words, counting the number of times a particular design occurs on a pot or on a painted frieze in a house may tell us virtually nothing of importance. What may be vital in understanding signification is whether two different designs can or cannot occur together on the rim of a pot or at the entrance to a house. Whether or not there are twenty depictions of one design type and six of another will usually be quite irrelevant. It is the rules of combination and relationality through a recognition of difference to which we need to pay attention.

Lévi-Strauss has defined the methodology involved as:

(1) define the phenomenon under study as a relation between two or more terms, real or supposed;
(2) construct a table of possible permutations between these terms;
(3) take this table as the general object of analysis which, at this level only, can yield necessary connections, the

21

empirical phenomenon considered at the beginning being
only one possible combination among others, the complete
system of which must be reconstructed beforehand.
(Lévi-Strauss 1962: 16)

We search for combinatorial rules through an analysis of empirical
phenomena and search for a system underlying them which must be
reconstructed beforehand through considering all permutational
possibilities of the terms or signs. We can then measure the degree
to which the real system diverges from the hypothetical system in
which all possible combinations are taken into account.

PARADIGMATIC SERIES
AND SYNTAGMATIC CHAINS

Signs, whether verbal or non-verbal, may be conceived as being
structured in two fundamentally different ways which are often not
simply a case of an either/or alternative. A paradigmatic series has
its basis in a recognition of similarity whereas a syntagmatic chain is
one based on contiguity or a set of spatial relations (Jakobson and
Halle 1956: 81). Other terms invoking this difference are metaphor
and metonymy. In the case of a paradigmatic or metaphoric
relationship between signs we assert similarity between a group of
signs. The easiest way to understand a metonymic relationship or a
syntagmatic chain is to think of a sentence. We can regard spoken
language as a code constituted by sound elements which convey
messages. Phonetic texts can be regarded in an analogous manner as
graphic elements (words) or signs which convey messages. In
spoken or written messages the elements of the message occur in
chains governed by rules of syntax. We can write in English 'the dog
is in the garden' but 'garden the in is dog the' makes no sense. Those
sentences that make sense can be referred to as syntagmatic chains in
which not only the differences between the words but their precise
spatial relationships to each other create the meaning. Meaning is
created by one part of the chain building on another in a definite
spatial order involving linearity.

In the *langue* of material culture we can distinguish a paradigmatic series as being made up by relations of affinity and a
syntagmatic chain as governing the manner in which the paradigmatic series is ordered 'on the ground'. To take the case of grave
goods, the paradigmatic series would be made up of variations in the

elements (types of pots, axes, beads, etc.). The syntagmatic chain would consist of sequences of these at the level of the grave. In designs on a pot we would have a contrast between motif-type variation, their occurrence or non-occurrence on particular areas of the pot surface (rim, neck, belly, base, etc.) constituting the paradigmatic series and their actual internal spatial arrangement from top to bottom or around the pot surface making up the syntagmatic chain. Barthes, somewhat confusingly using the terms 'system' and 'syntagm', provides other examples. For instance, in the *langue* of garments or clothing we can distinguish between sets of pieces which cannot be worn at the same time on the same part of the body and whose variation corresponds to a change in meaning (beret/bowler hat), while the syntagmatic chain consists of juxta-position in the same type of dress of different elements (skirt, blouse, jacket) (see Barthes 1984: 125 and Olsen 1990 for other examples).

EDITING THE BOOK

Hallström mentions 'literature' and 'reading', the carvings at Nämforsen as text. The problem becomes, of course, how the 'text' of Nämforsen is to be read. The text to hand consists solely of visual imagery, something both more and less than graphic marks on a page. To read Nämforsen, unlike reading a book, is to write it. This reading is a process of translation, the movement from things to words, imagery to language. The book of Nämforsen is torn up and floating around in a river. A first requirement must be to piece it back together by defining the constitutive units of the visual text, the 'words', the 'sentences' or syntactical relations in which the words occur, and the 'pages' on which these meaning units are set out.

As in a book, the pages will be obviously and clearly differentiated in a physical sense. A page is bounded by margins, is numbered, and one must turn it to move onto the next. Pages, although recognized at a glance, are entirely arbitrary. The number of sentences on a page depends on lettering and page size etc. The sentence sequence is linear and that which is the last sentence, on any particular page, does not matter. It is, of course, necessary to be both empirical and nominalist and this beginning – conceived as an ending – has been made in a most thorough fashion by Hallström. He divided the rock carving surfaces into three main groups. Two of these, situated on

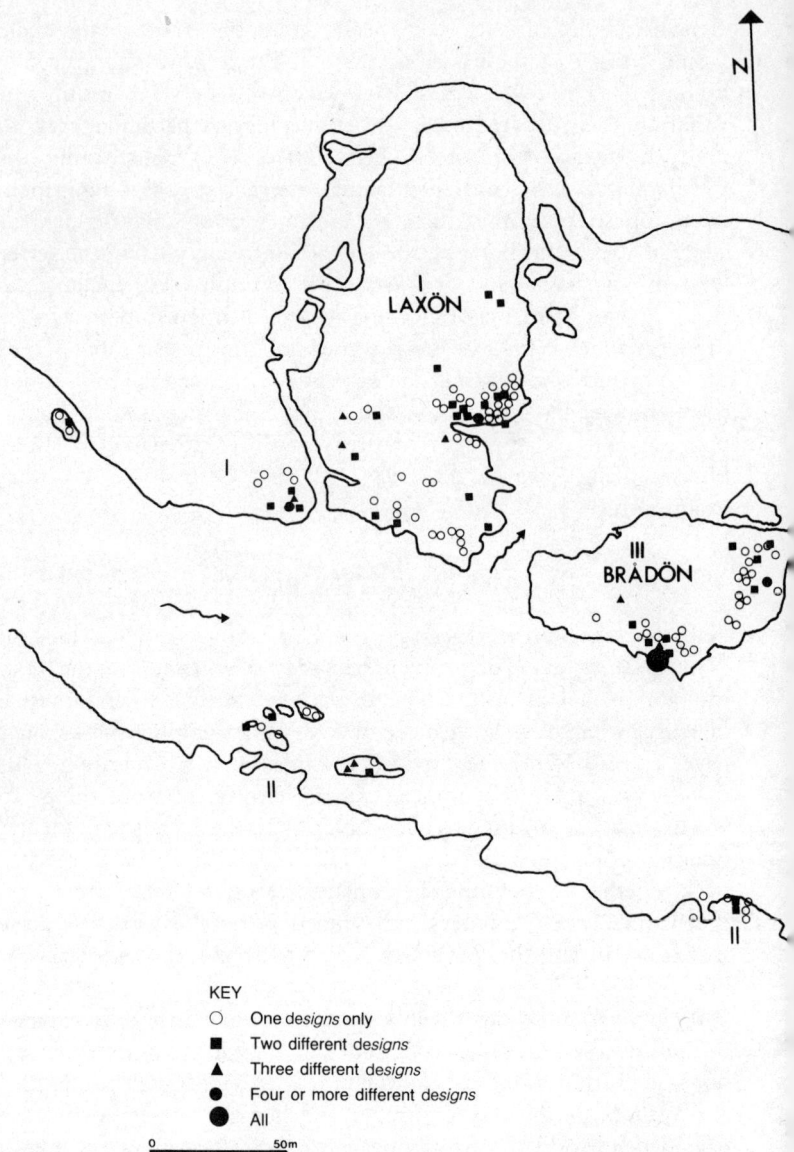

Figure 11 The rock carving surfaces at Nämforsen according to qualitative occurrence of *design* relationships. Topographical carving pages and the contemporary settlement are marked

IV
NOTÖN

II

SETTLEMENT

the islands of Notön and Brådön in the river channel, are clearly defined topographically. The third consists of carvings on the island of Laxön (artificially created by blasting and originally forming part of the northern river bank), and the northern and southern river banks. In what follows I regroup the rock carving surfaces into four topographically defined units:

    I The northern river shore
   II The southern river shore
  III The western island, Brådön
  IV The eastern island, Notön (Figure 11)

These units, we might say, constitute the pages of Nämforsen. They all have watery margins and are clearly separated from each other. Naturally, the numbers that have been given to these pages are entirely arbitrary. Depending on where you stand at Nämforsen, on the islands or the river banks, the pages may be ordered differently. However, it is interesting to note that the carvings on page I (the northern river shore) occur furthest to the west along the longitudinal axis of the river channel, while those on page II occur furthest to the east. The river course is a channel of movement, of water flow, of passage. If we were to assume that the text of Nämforsen is linear, that the second page builds on the first, and so on, then the page sequence becomes less arbitrary. The pages, or topographically defined units, must be reordered as I, III, IV, II or vice versa. We know which the middle pages are but remain uncertain as to the beginning or end of the text.

From pages to the syntax of relational meaning units: Hallström divided the totality of the rock carvings into 262 separate carving surfaces. As far as I can reconstruct his method, four main criteria appear to have been used.

A rock carving surface is

(i) an individual unbroken rock surface.
(ii) Cleavages or other natural breaks such as ridges between rock surfaces sloping in different directions on a single rock surface or area of conjoined carved rocks may be used to define two or more units on the same or different rock surfaces, if the carved area is very large.
(iii) Large gaps or spaces between clusters of designs may be used to define separate carving surfaces.
(iv) Date of discovery: Hallström sometimes differentiates between

subgroups on the basis of convenience. If a subgroup has already been defined and drawn and later another figure is discovered nearby this may be assigned a different number.

I have followed Hallström in most of his unit definitions based on criteria i–iii above while omitting surfaces without identifiable designs and regrouping most of those he differentiates between for the sake of convenience (point iv above). It is important to point out that ultimately any division of the material at Nämforsen into separate units remains arbitrary and cannot be finally justified. It is not and cannot be objective. It can only be more or less consistent. By dividing up the material we are already constructing a past in the present, a construction on which we may then set to work. The division of the material does not claim to be any more objective than Hallström's. It is just different: my (partial) creation rather than his. I subdivide the material into 234 units by main group or page as follows: I 69; II 26; III 38; IV 101. These constitute the sentences or meaning units of which the site is composed.

Each of these units is composed of one or more carved or pecked motifs forming a bundle of relations within and between units. The next stage is to single out the words or signs from which these relational units may be built up. The words at Nämforsen are all visual images or motifs or designs. This last word 'design' will prove of particular use in what follows if I transform it into de*sign*. By doing this I intend a certain compression of meaning: the visual design as a design and the design as equivalent to a linguistic sign involving a diacritical relation between a signifier (the visual image) and that which it signifies (a concept or thing). In the visual language of Nämforsen any de*sign* may signify 'itself' or something other. So the de*sign* of an elk may mean the hoofed animal elk, or something quite different, or take on a multiplicity of different meanings according to context.

One striking feature of the carved de*signs* at Nämforsen is that they appear to be almost entirely representational. Abstract patterns such as zig-zag lines, spirals or circles (with one important exception discussed below) do not occur. Seven major classes of de*signs* can be identified: animals, fish, birds, boats, tools (two main types: scythe-like implements and elk-head 'axes' or elk heads on poles), shoe soles and human beings (Figure 12). It is of interest to know what types of animals, fish or birds are being depicted. In identifying the de*signs* we are, in effect, identifying the signifiers and this may tell

27

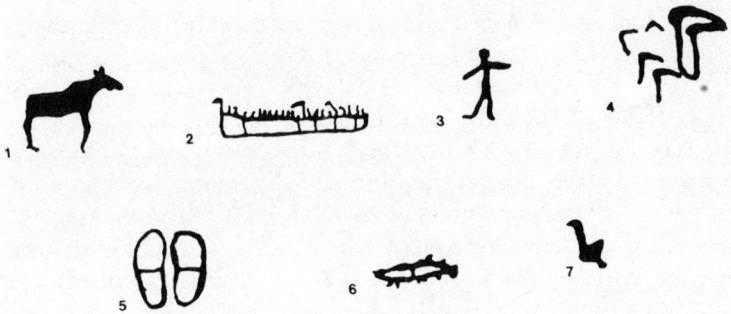

Figure 12 The main types of designs at Nämforsen. 1: elk; 2: boat; 3: human; 4: tool; 5: shoe sole; 6: fish; 7: bird

us nothing about signification or meaning since the relationship between a signifier and a signified remains entirely arbitrary within a language. But we need to remember that Nämforsen is not a real text but a material text and consequently the relation between signifier and signified may be considerably more restricted or indeed take on a rather different nature.

The only animal species that can be identified with any certainty is the elk. The more naturalistic depictions possess a number of characteristics such as body shape, head shape and hanging muzzle which clearly mark the figures as elks. Other more stylized depictions might represent other types of hoofed animals but there is a complete lack of any positive evidence for a determination other than elk. I agree with Hallström that reindeer are absent and that 'the great majority of the animal figures are intended to represent elks' (Hallström 1960: 291). He suggests that in two cases dogs might be identified and in a further five or six possibly bears (Hallström 1960: 291). However, the identification of the latter two species remains thoroughly ambiguous and can be disputed. Since elks are in many cases depicted with considerable skill it seems safe to assume that the same technical competence might be used to depict other species unambiguously. It is, however, this very ambiguity that is important and needs to be understood. In connection with the last point it is particularly interesting to note that distinct species of fish (apart from salmon) or other species living in water, such as seals or porpoises, are also impossible to recognize. Water-inhabiting birds such as swans or cranes appear to be depicted but again it is not possible to recognize any individual species.

28

BREAKING DOWN THE TEXT

Up to this point Nämforsen has not been read at all. I have constituted the text that is to be read in terms of pages, relational meaning units and de*signs* making up these meaning units and pages. Now that the book has been edited, the next stage is to begin to read it. A start can be made by exploring the de*signs* a little further. Their distribution is shown in Table 1.

Table 1 The distribution of de*signs* at Nämforsen in relation to pages (topographical units)

Design	Page I		Page II		Page III		Page IV		Total
	n	%	n	%	n	%	n	%	
elks	238	35	27	4	193	29	213	32	671
boats	40	12	49	15	28	8	220	65	337
humans	30	33	–	–	11	12	51	55	92
fish	8	42	2	11	7	37	2	11	19
birds	3	33	–	–	3	33	3	33	9
shoe soles	5	16	–	–	25	81	1	3	31
tools	24	37	7	11	3	5	30	47	64
Total	348		85		270		520		1,223
Total %	28		7		22		43		

In total Hallström lists *c.* 1,750 different figures including *c.* 34 cup-shaped hollows and *c.* 375 depictions he cannot identify. A further *c.* 300 carved lines are taken to be either beginnings or remains of designs bringing the overall total to around 2,000 (1960: 283). The figures given in Table 1 for different classes of representational de*signs* differ from those given by Hallström: his are higher within each class because he 'sees' more in the carved surfaces than I am able to do from the plates provided in his publication. Malmer (1981: Tables) 'sees' less: the absolute figures do not matter and we can expect a different result from any individual archaeologist who might care to study Hallström's plates, or indeed (perhaps even more so) the original carvings. It is possible to agree with both Hallström and Malmer, that the main types of representational de*signs* are those listed above, that depictions of animals dominate, and that distribution of different types of de*signs* varies considerably according to the main groups or pages I–IV above.

It is apparent that about 65 per cent of the de*signs* occur on islands in the rapids. Those along the river banks, especially the southern river bank, are fewer: only four of the seven main classes occur. Boats predominate on page II, occur in roughly equal numbers with animals on page IV and are comparatively few on pages I and III, where animals dominate. Humans are infrequently depicted in comparison with animals and boats, being most common on pages I and IV. Fish and birds are uncommon, while shoe soles only occur in any quantity on page III. Tools cluster on pages I and IV. So there is considerable variability in the quantitative occurrence of different types of de*signs* from one rock carving area to another, but in all cases either animals or boats dominate. These are by far the most important signs in the de*sign* surfaces, by comparison with which humanity becomes a pale shadow, a shadow entirely absent on the southern river banks.

INVESTIGATING THE GRAMMAR

Signs on pages, but what of the grammar? Can we distinguish a generative structure for the de*signs*? In this section I wish to investigate associations between different types of de*sign* on individual rock carving surfaces. I am asking: What kinds of combinations occur? What are the permissible limits of de*sign* combination? Do these combinations differ over space? A certain degree of simplification is essential for the analysis to be manageable. I am concerned at this stage only with 'free-standing' de*signs* so, for example, if tools occur on their own they are counted as constitutive de*signs* in their own right, but if held by a human body they are not.

The simplest rock carving surfaces consist of those with only one isolated de*sign* or variable numbers of the same kind, e.g. boats. From Table 2 and Figures 13–16 it is evident that some 60 per cent of all carving surfaces possess only one de*sign* type, most of these being either elks or boats.

Birds are never depicted on their own, but in view of absolute numbers this may not be significant. Considering the small overall numbers of fish de*signs* a surprisingly large number (42 per cent) occur on their own or solely in combination with other fish. Shoe soles occur only once on their own and tools are rarely depicted in isolation. The really striking feature of this table is the absence of humanity. Humans, with one possible exception, are never found as isolated depictions. When one considers that human bodies are the

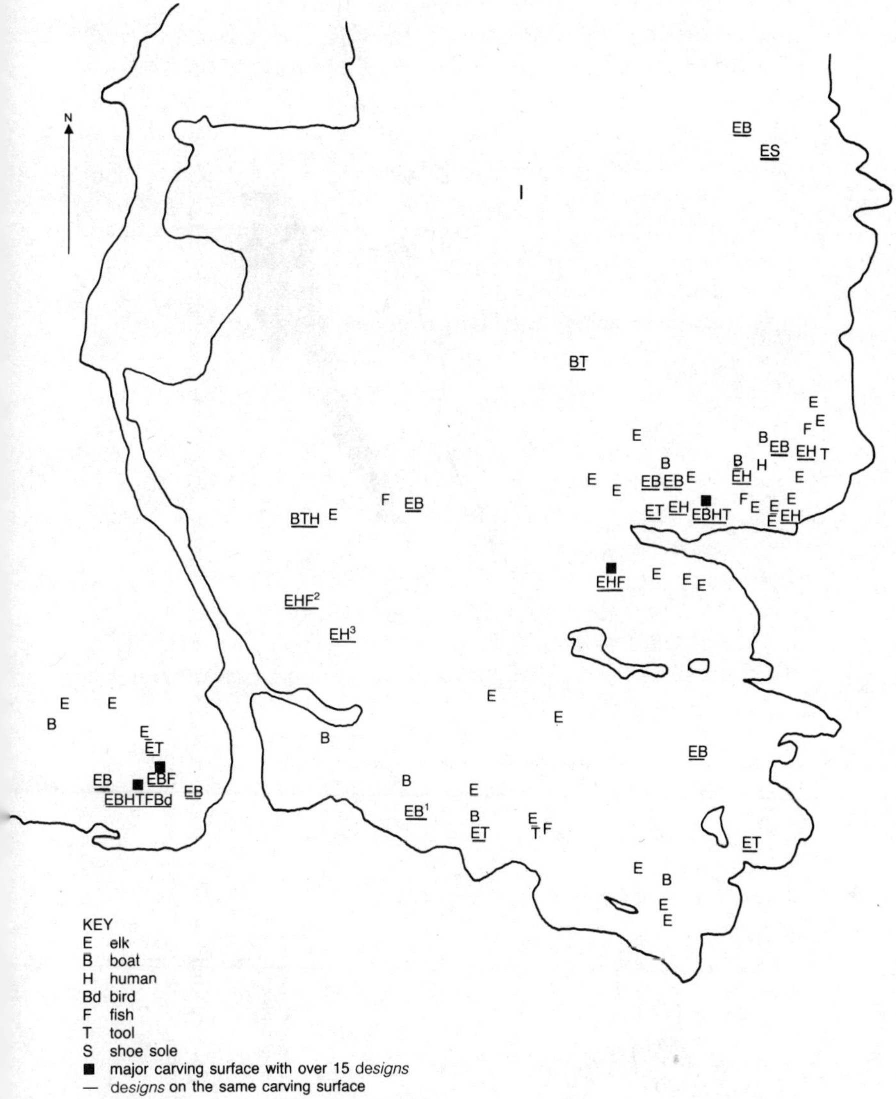

KEY
E   elk
B   boat
H   human
Bd bird
F   fish
T   tool
S   shoe sole
■   major carving surface with over 15 designs
—   designs on the same carving surface

Figure 13 Carving surfaces on page I (northern river banks) according to the qualitative occurrence of different types of de*signs* on the same carving surface. Numbers refer to other figure captions in the text

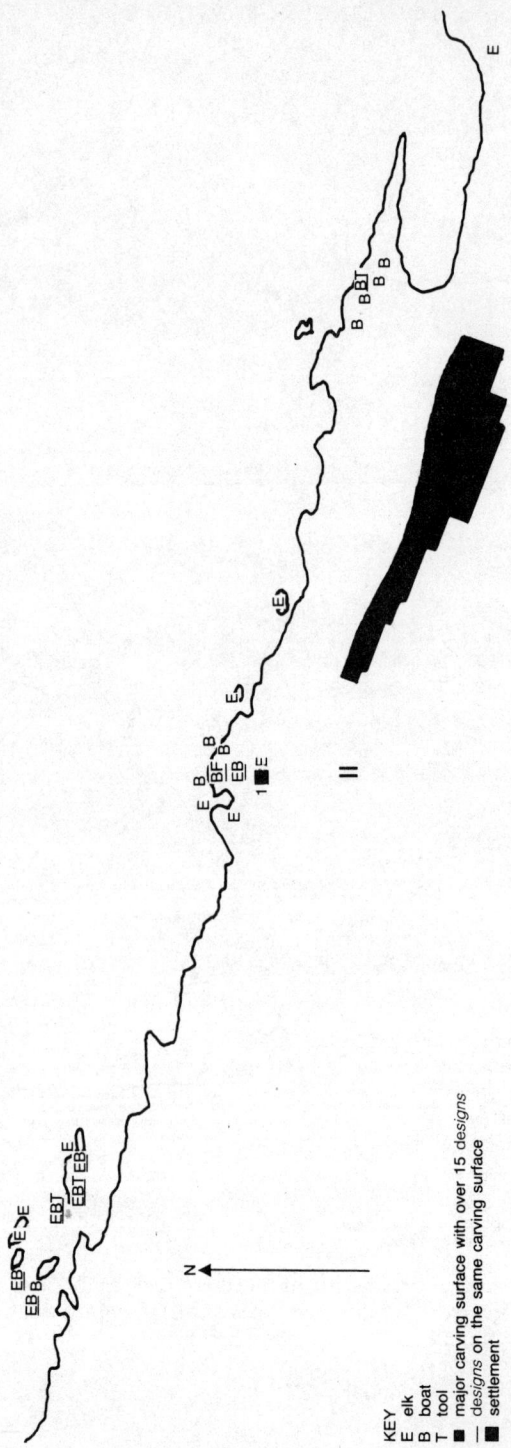

KEY
E elk
B boat
T tool
■ major carving surface with over 15 *designs*
— *designs* on the same carving surface
■ settlement

Figure 14 Carving surfaces on page II (southern river banks) according to the qualitative occurrence of different types of *designs*. Numbers refer to other figure captions in the text

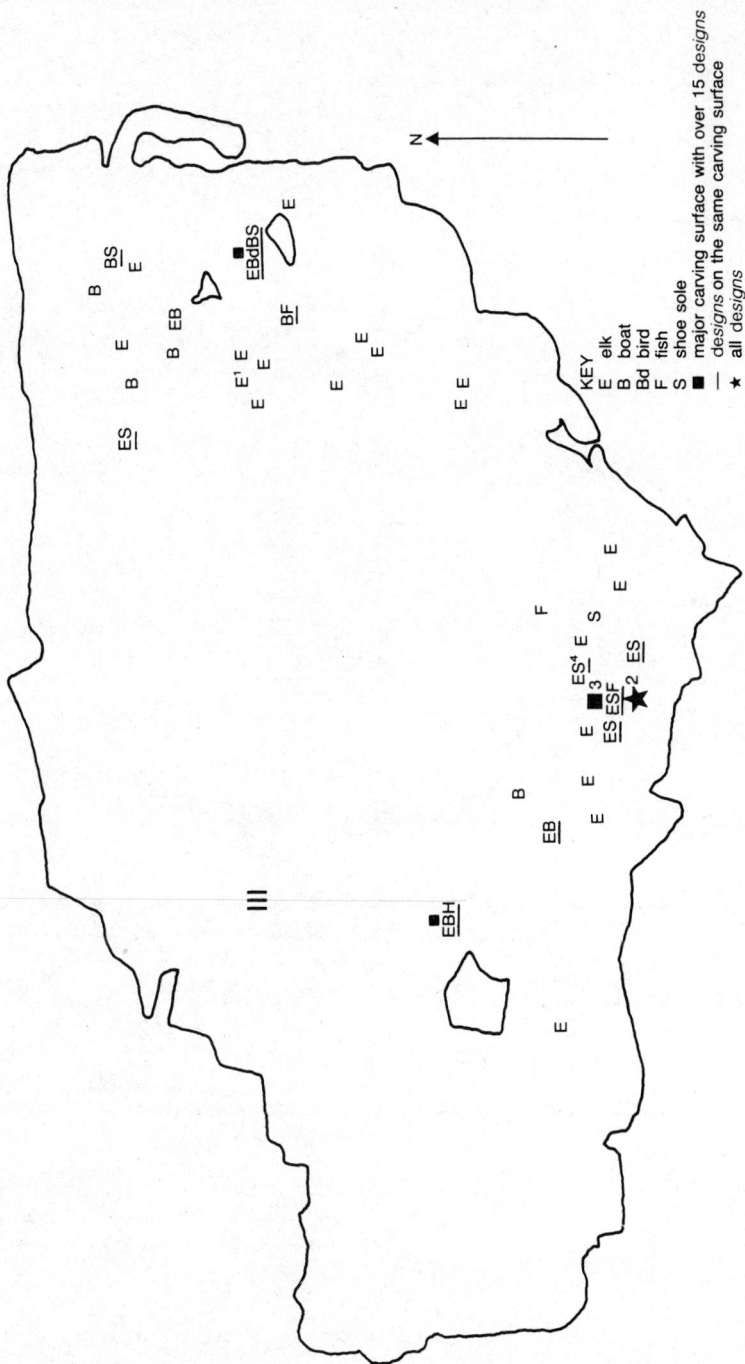

Figure 15 Carving surfaces on page III (Brådön) according to the qualitative occurrence of different types of designs. Numbers refer to other figure captions in the text

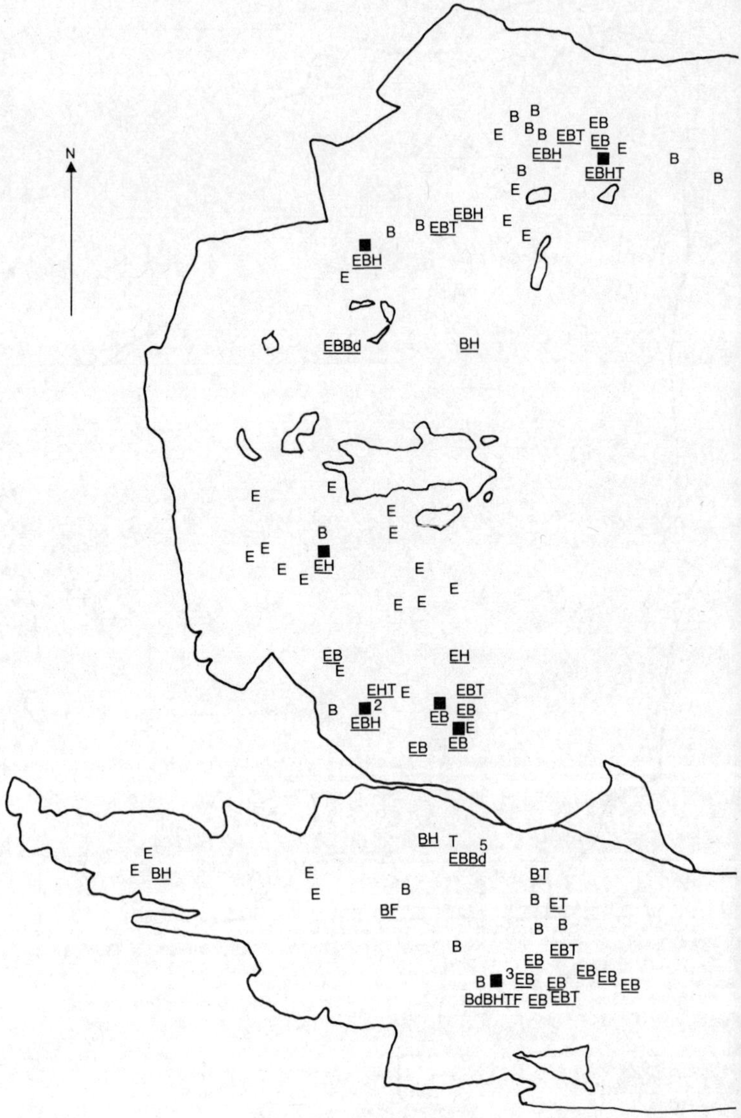
N
B B
E B B EBT EB
EB E
EBH
B B
EBHT
B
E
EBH
B EBT E
E
EBH
E
EBBd BH
E E
E
B E
E E
EH
E E
E
E E E
EB EH
E
EHT E EBT
B 2 EBH EB EB E EB
EB
BH T 5 EBBd
E E BH E BT
E B B ET
BF B B
B EBT
EB
B 3 EB EB EB EB EB
BdBHTF EB EBT

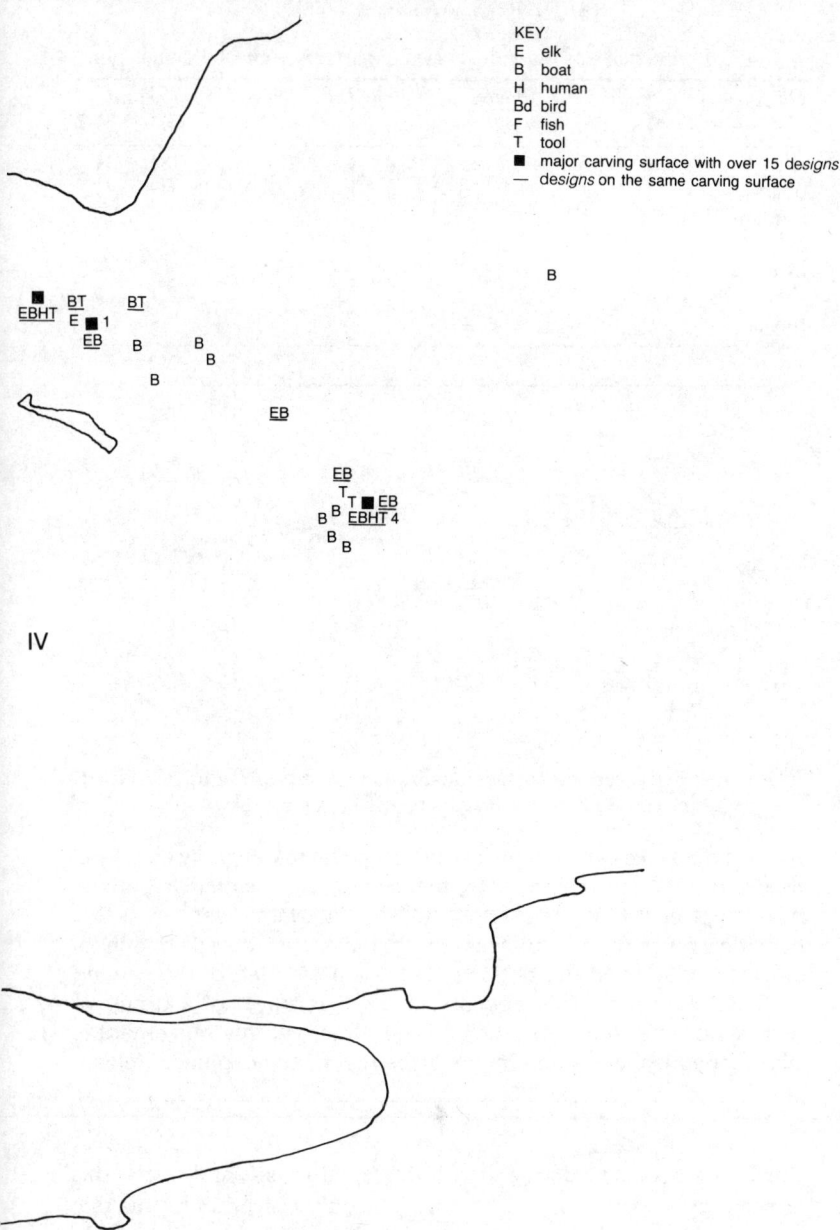

KEY
E   elk
B   boat
H   human
Bd   bird
F   fish
T   tool
■   major carving surface with over 15 designs
—   designs on the same carving surface

Figure 16 Carving surfaces on page IV (Notön) according to the qualitative occurrence of different types of designs on the same carving surface. Numbers refer to other figure captions in the text

Table 2 Frequencies of individual carving surfaces with one de*sign* type

Design	Page I		Page II		Page III		Page IV		Total	
	n	%	n	%	n	%	n	%	n	%
elks	26	37	9	35	19	49	27	28	81	34
boats	9	12	9	35	4	11	27	28	49	21
humans	1?	1	–	–	–	–	–	–	1?	–
fish	4	5	–	–	1	3	–	–	5	2
birds	–	–	–	–	–	–	–	–	–	–
shoe soles	–	–	–	–	1	3	–	–	1	–
tools	2	3	–	–	–	–	3	3	5	2
Total	42	58	18	70	25	66	57	59	142	59

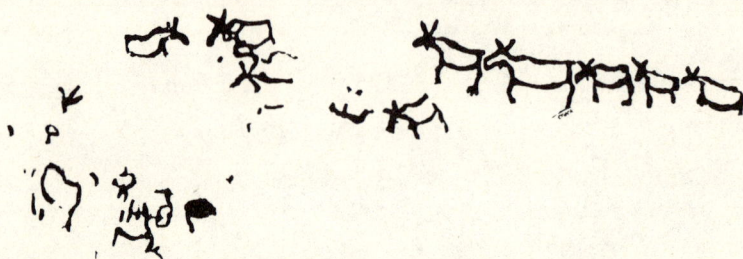

Figure 17 Rock carving surface on Brådön (Location Figure 15, No. 1. Source: Hallström 1960: Plate XXVI: O:2. Scale: 1:20

At least nine elks can now be identified on this rather badly damaged rock surface. All the clearly identifiable animals are carved in outline. As is typical for many carving surfaces at Nämforsen on which considerable numbers of elks are depicted, a straggling line of animals is depicted. All but one, to the extreme left of the carving surface, face right. This appears to be a portrayal of a group of animals on the move, one behind the other, yet this movement is simultaneously arrested. The legs seem stiff, static, glued, lifeless.

third most frequent de*sign* at Nämforsen after elks and boats, this appears to be even more significant. The only exception to this rule (Figure 18), with headdress unique for Nämforsen (cf. humans in Figures 5–7, 19 and 33), actually appears to be a depiction of a deity rather than a normal human figure.

We can now examine rock carving surfaces on which two

Figure 18 The only 'human' figure to occur in isolation, northern river banks (Photo: Michael Shanks)

different de*sign* forms occur. Given that we have seven classes of de*signs* (see Table 2 and Figure 12), there are in all twenty-one possible different combinations. In fact only eight or 38 per cent of these de*sign* combinations occur (Table 3). The permissible limits of de*sign* combination appear to be rather strictly confined and differ according to main de*sign* group. Tools (as separate depictions rather than held in the hand by a human figure) are only combined with elks or boats, as are shoe soles. Humans may only be combined with elks or boats and not with tools, shoe soles, fish or birds. The birds are again not combined in a pair with any other de*sign* category.

Table 3 Combinations of two de*signs* on individual carving surfaces in relation to topographical units or pages

Design *combination*	Page I		Page II		Page III		Page IV		Total	
	n	%	n	%	n	%	n	%	n	%
elks and boats	10	15	4	15	2	5	19	19	35	15
elks and tools	4	6	–	–	–	–	1	1	5	2
elks and shoe soles	1	1	–	–	4	12	–	–	5	2
elks and humans	5	8	–	–	–	–	3	3	8	4
boats and tools	1	1	1	4	–	–	3	3	5	2
boats and shoe soles	–	–	–	–	1	3	–	–	1	–
boats and humans	–	–	–	–	–	–	2	2	2	1
boats and fish	–	–	1	4	1	3	1	1	3	1
Total	21	31	6	23	8	23	29	29	64	27

An isolated de*sign* or variable numbers of the same de*sign* type and combinations of two different de*signs* (each with variable frequencies, e.g. there may be three elks and one boat) account for 206 or 88 per cent of the carving surfaces at Nämforsen. There are twenty rock carving surfaces on which three different de*signs* occur (Table 4). A total of thirty-five de*sign* combinations are logically possible whereas only eight or 23 per cent are actually utilized.

Combination possibilities are very strictly delimited. Humanity makes a much more frequent appearance than hitherto, occurring in three of the four de*sign* combinations. Elks occur in seven of the de*sign* combinations, boats in five. Again, de*sign* combinations differ according to topographical page.

Only eight different carving surfaces possess more than three

Table 4 Frequency of combinations of three different designs on the carving surfaces according to topographical pages

Design combination	Page I	Page II	Page III	Page IV	Total
elks, boats, tools	–	2	–	5	7
elks, boats, humans	–	–	1	4	5
boats, tools, humans	1	–	–	–	1
elks, humans, fish	2	–	–	–	2
elks, shoe sole, fish	–	–	1	–	1
elks, boat, fish	1	–	–	–	1
elks, boat, bird	–	–	–	2	2
elks, human, tool	–	–	–	1	1
Total	4	2	2	12	20

different design combinations and these are listed in Table 5. In only one case do all the different designs occur together on one carving surface, on page III, the island of Brådön. Brådön (see Figure 11) is positioned more or less exactly in the centre of the Nämforsen rock carving area. The rock carving surface on which all the designs occur together is moreover roughly at the central point in the distribution of rock carvings on the island (Figure 15). Furthermore, it is the rock carving surface with the greatest number of individual designs (over 100 figures). It is on this rock carving surface that a unique design occurs not encountered elsewhere at Nämforsen: a circle enclosing a cross (see Figure 19). This so-called 'sun wheel' has been interpreted as evidence of contact with the southern Scandinavian Bronze Age cultural tradition. Irrespective of whether or not this is the case, its position on just this rock surface would appear to be no

Table 5 Frequency of combinations of more than three different designs on the carving surfaces according to topographical pages

Design combination	Page I	Page II	Page III	Page IV
elk, boat, human, tool	1	–	–	3
elk, bird, boat, shoe sole	–	–	1	–
boat, human, tool, fish, bird	–	–	–	1
elk, boat, human, tool, fish, bird	1	–	–	–
all designs	–	–	1	–
Total	2	–	2	4

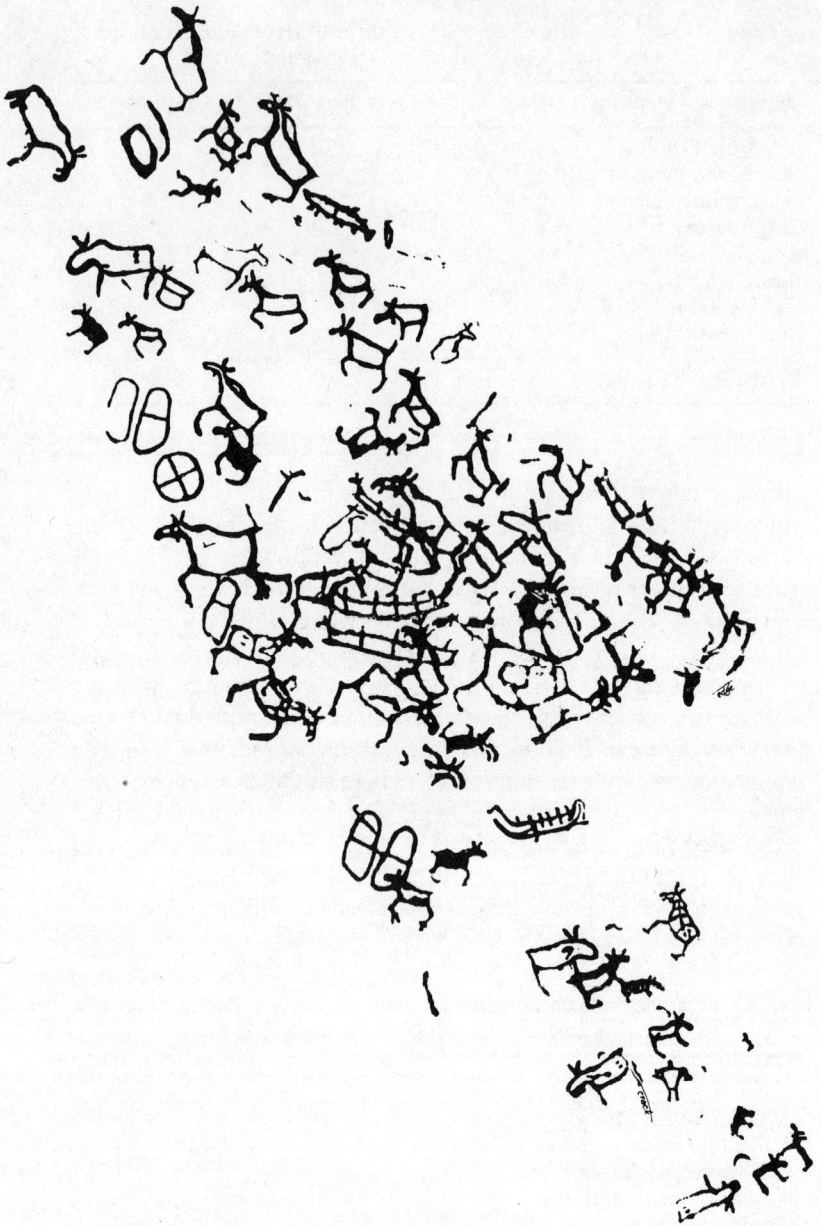

Figure 19 Brådön: the central rock carving surface (Location: Figure 15, No. 2 and see also Figure 11. Source: Hallström: Plate XXV: E: 4–6. Scale: 1:20).

mere accident. I suggest it marks the centre of the rock carving area, not only physically but also as the only point where all de*signs* come together in combination.

The text of Nämforsen, we might say, reaches its 'conclusion' in

---

This is one of the best preserved carving surfaces at Nämforsen and the only one on which all seven major de*sign* forms occur together along with a unique non-representational de*sign*: a cross in a circle. Additionally this carving surface portrays numerically the greatest number of motifs: at least fifty-seven elks, one bird, one fish, two humans, five boats, three tools, five to six shoe soles and one elk head on a pole. It is the only carving surface on which humans are depicted in both scooped and outline technique with 'triangular' bodies. It is also the only surface on which outline elks are depicted with an internal networking of lines inside the body. Located at the centre of the entire rock carving area, everything comes together here, both physically and in terms of de*sign* representation. However, this carving surface, like the others at Nämforsen, lacks any clear boundaries and has no obvious central point. The circle–cross is one candidate for a central point or the elk head on a pole immediately to the right but both are clearly off-centre in a west–east direction. As we might expect, it is overlapping and entwined boats and elks that occur at the heart of this carving surface.

Virtually all the elks appear highly active, a writhing mass of bodies. There is no indication of any degree of linearity in their relationship (cf. Figure 33). Some face west, others east, others are orientated north–west or south–east. A few appear 'upside down'. There is a tremendous degree of overlap between elk bodies and between the elks and the three double lined boats (possessing elk-head prows) in the middle. As we move out from the elks and boats in the middle, the degree of de*sign* overlap diminishes. The fish and bird to the top right are not superpositioned, nor are the two human figures at the extreme north–west and south–east terminations. Only one elk overlaps part of a pair of shoe soles.

As on so many other occasions at Nämforsen, human bodies lacking any indications of sex are both isolated (they do not overlap with other depictions) and in marginal positions: they are merely traces at the edges of the carving surface. Apart from this one depiction, the human body in 'triangular' form at the bottom only occurs elsewhere on the island of Notön. In this 'display' of all the elements to be encountered at Nämforsen it is the elks and boats that take centre-stage and together, or alone, they are never to lose it.

the middle. But this conclusion has to be understood in the special sense of a carving surface in which the totality of the grammatically possible relations between the de*signs* are brought together, the only carving surface on which every de*sign* occurs together with every other de*sign*. A text that concludes in the middle is, of course, rather unusual but then Nämforsen is no ordinary text. It is both something more and something less.

4

WHY NÄMFORSEN?

This is a question of signification. The de*signs* at Nämforsen are limited in number and their combinational possibilities on individual carving surfaces restricted. By considering these combinations I have attempted to reconstruct a relational de*sign* grammar which determines that which may or may not occur. But what does this generative grammar mean? Is it possible to understand it? The first and most obvious possibility is that a de*sign* means itself and this is the manner in which archaeologists have virtually universally interpreted the rock carvings at Nämforsen and indeed throughout Scandinavia and Europe. By employing the concept of the de*sign* and in discussing Hallström's work, I have already called into question such a simple equation but it needs to be considered further. Does it lead us anywhere?

SIGNIFICATION THROUGH
DENOTATION AND CONNOTATION

Denotation and connotation make up two different ways of signifying meaning. The major difference is that connotation is more indirect, building on a previously established denotative process of signification. In a general sense any system of signification involves: (1) a plane of expression, the medium through which it takes place [E]; (2) a plane of content [C], with the process of signification coinciding with the relation of these two planes [R] (Barthes 1984: 149). This is merely a way of restating the diacritical signifier/signified relation and can be termed a denotative process of signification. Connotative signification occurs when this system E R C itself serves as a basis for a second system parasitic on the initial denotative level and wider than it:

2	E	R	C
1	ERC		

The initial denotative plane of signification transforms into a connotative level. That which has the status of a sign in the first level becomes simply a signifier at the second level. To put this more simply at the level of language, denotative signification is when we take a sentence to mean what it says, connotative signification is when a sentence means something other than what is actually said or written. Connotation is particularly prevalent in 'literary' writing, graphic forms, iconography and the use of signs (symbols) in arenas of social life such as ritual.

Following Pierce (discussed in Eco 1976) we can also use another terminology and attempt to distinguish between iconical, indexical and symbolic signs. An icon is something that signifies by virtue of its resemblance to its object. For example, I depict a snake and the relationship between this depiction and that signified is more or less direct. However, this does not necessarily mean that the depiction of a snake only signifies that creature and nothing else, i.e. remains on the level of denotation. An index signifies by virtue of some kind of empirical or cause–effect relationship with its object. Example: smoke is an index of fire. In the symbol the relationship between signifier and signified is arbitrary in the sense that there is no natural connection and the interpreter has to make it. A single sign may combine iconological, indexical and symbolic properties and work simultaneously on denotative and connotative levels. The different levels are not mutually exclusive and there may be varying degrees of condensation of meaning in the same form. This is typical of the Nämforsen carvings.

DENOTATION AND FUNCTIONAL MEANING

The rock carvings of Scandinavia (Figure 20) have traditionally been divided into two main groups, a southern one associated with a Bronze Age farming population and a northern one produced by hunter–fisher–gatherers. Nämforsen belongs to the latter group. Geographically, the site may be held to be part of a rather scattered series of northern Swedish rock carving and painting sites (Figure 21). The nearest distances between Nämforsen and the closest sites in this group are *c.* 60 km to the west and *c.* 70 km to the east. It is *c.* 400 km from the nearest Swedish rock carving area to the south.

Figure 20   Major areas with rock carvings/paintings in Scandinavia

In connection with the regulation of lake and river systems and the building of hydroelectric power plants since the late 1930s a vast number of archaeological sites have been located and documented in northern Sweden with numbers reaching *c.* 3,000. Within the Ångerman river system alone over 600 are now known (Janson and Hvarfner 1966; Baudou 1977: 68; Figure 22) and there is a considerable concentration of sites along the river courses and lake systems

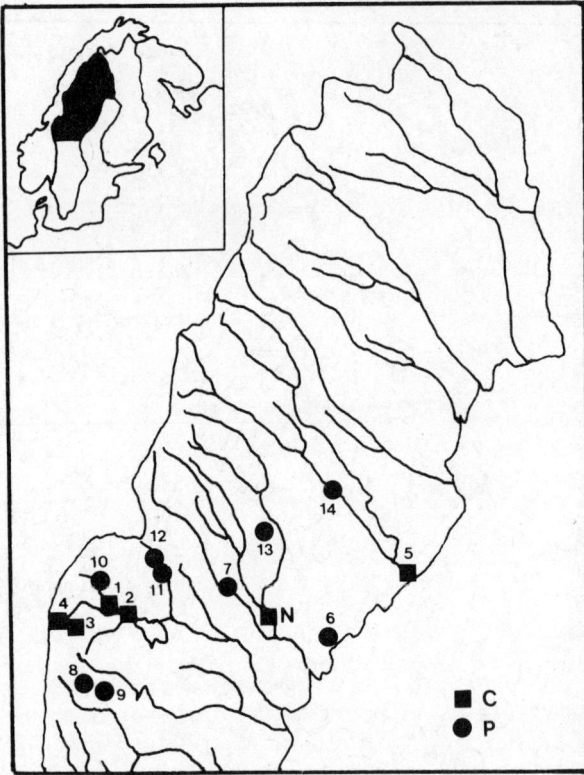

Figure 21   Rock carving and painting sites in northern Sweden. C: carving
site; P: painting site (After Ramqvist, Forsberg and Backe 1985: Figure 1)

immediately above Nämforsen. Most sites lack any stratigraphy and
preservation conditions are generally poor. Only burnt bone fragments are preserved. The majority of sites consist of discontinuous
scatters of artefacts and waste materials in thin horizons of leached,
podzolic soil. As we might expect from the rock carvings, the most
important animal species represented in the little bone material
which is preserved is the elk, followed by beaver. A detailed
quantitative analysis of the material has been carried out by Ekman
and Iregren (1983) who identified seventeen mammal, fourteen bird
and eight fish species in the northern Swedish data taken as a whole.
Remains relating to mammal hunting occurred on virtually all sites
(99 per cent), birds on 17 per cent and fishing on 34 per cent (Ekman
and Iregren 1983: 31). The southern limit of the now extinct wild

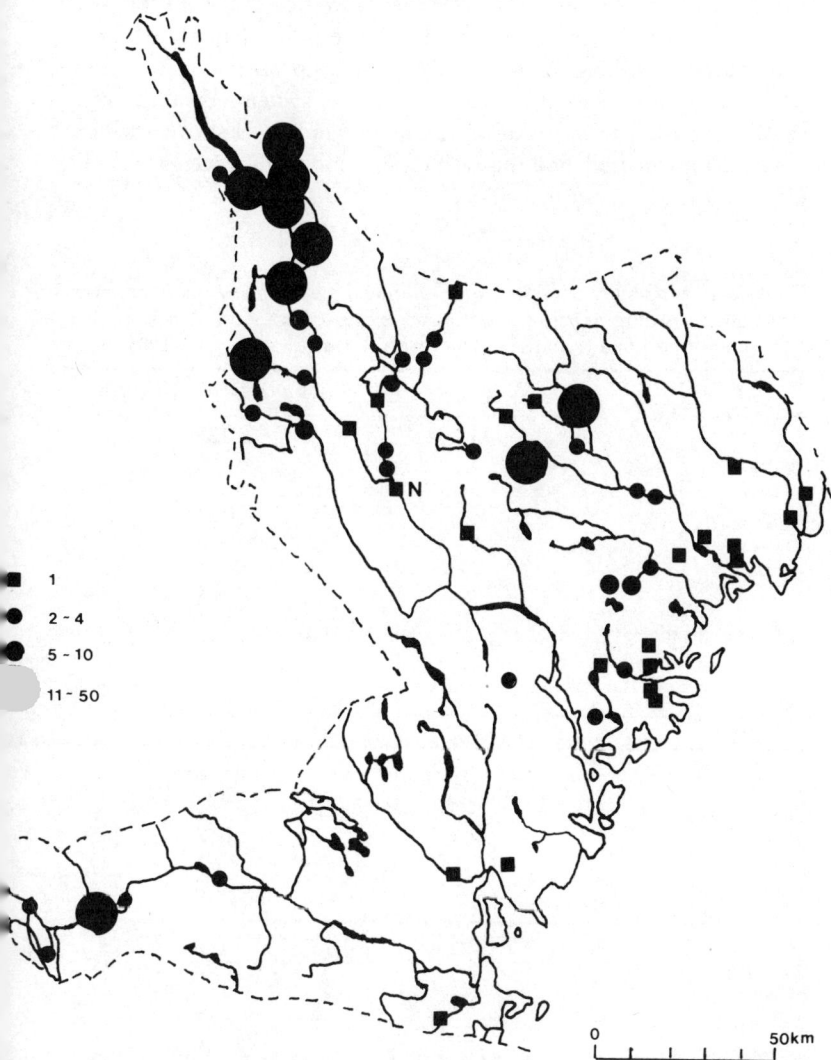

Figure 22 Frequencies of recorded prehistoric settlement sites in Ångermanland county, northern Sweden. Nämforsen is marked. (After Baudou 1977: Figure 34)

reindeer appears to have been along the Ångerman river, where faunal remains from sites constituted only a very small sample of the faunal material, and increases significantly northwards on sites along other river systems. Ekman and Iregren estimate that only three mammal species, elk, reindeer and beaver, were of any economic importance in prehistoric northern Sweden and of these elk made up at least 75 per cent of the total meat coming from mammals (p. 38). Along the Ångerman river system elk and beaver totally dominate in terms of bone counts, number of sites on which they are represented, and the former in terms of meat weight (Table 6).

Table 6 Burnt bone materials from the inland area of the Ångerman river system according to representation on excavated sites and numbers of identified bone fragments. Data from Ekman and Iregren 1983

Species	No. of sites	No. of burnt bone fragments
elk	43	2,175
reindeer	5	16
beaver	26	4,924
bear	6	13
marten	5	188
otter	1	1
wolf	1	6
fox	1	1
dog	2	28
hare	3	7
seal	3	79
sheep/goat	2	2
cattle	1	2
black-headed diver	1	1
goose	1	1
swan	2	2
crane	1	1
capercaillie	4	30
black grouse	3	10
pike	14	136
bream	6	22
perch	2	6
whitefish	2	17
salmon	3	31
ide	1	1

One of the largest of the known settlements along the Ångerman river system is on the southern river banks at Nämforsen stretching over an area of at least 120 m in length and *c*. 20 m in width (Figure 11). According to Baudou this site was discontinuously occupied from the Neolithic (*c*. 3000 BC) to the Iron Age (it should be pointed out that Neolithic in this context does not necessarily imply agriculture). It was thus occupied during the period in which the rocks were carved. There is no structural evidence and about 90 per cent of the material consists of quartz waste from tool working, flakes and chips, along with thirty arrowheads or points and up to 600 broken projectile point pieces. Among 6 kg of potsherds, mostly of grey asbestos type, a few pieces have imitation textile ornamentation datable to the early Bronze Age (Baudou 1977: 72–4). From very small quantities of burnt and unburnt bone, the species recorded were salmon, beaver, pike, ide and one seal bone. Of great interest is the absence of elk bones.

The huge accumulation of rock carvings at this site, together with its relative isolation, northerly location, and connection with a hunter–gatherer–fisher economy, has attracted much discussion, which has centred on (a) the interpretation of the carved motifs; (b) the location of the site. As regards the first question little has been done beyond the identification of motif types. Explanations of why particular types of designs were carved bear a striking resemblance to those purporting to explain Palaeolithic cave art (see Ucko and Rosenfeld 1967). They have almost exclusively focused on some variant of a sympathetic magic hypothesis and reference has also been made to functionalist theories of animal totemism (for recent examples dealing with other northern Scandinavian rock carving localities see also Simonsen 1986; Mikkelsen 1986). It is primarily only one type of *design*, the elk, that has been explained in this manner. Elks are depicted in order to maintain magical control over them and facilitate the hunt and/or to ensure their fertility and increase, in which human groups play an important symbolic role. The elk is the animal species depicted because of its dietary importance and it also perhaps was a totemic emblem for the people carving it. This is a logical consequence of economic necessity. Because the elk was a critical resource for those populations dependent on it, the adoption of the elk as a totemic symbol would follow as a natural consequence. Human culture is grounded in biological necessity.

These ideas have been coupled with consideration of the location of Nämforsen at the site of a violent series of rapids:

The Nämforsen carvings tell us that the elk was the most desirable prey in the hunting activity. How the hunt was performed we do not know more than the rapids must have constituted its finishing moment. ... The violent rapids and the precipitous 'nipas' (river banks, here 60 m high) were good instruments in such a method. A nowadays visitor, being rowed upstream to the islands, might easily visualize the brutal effectivity of old-time hunters and get visions of small catching boats among whirling dead and halfdead animal bodies.

(Hallström 1960: 377)

Janson (1966: 39–40; Janson and Janson 1980: 9) makes virtually identical remarks, while according to Malmer:

This is a natural place for these rock carvings depicting game and hunting, and probably with a magic purpose. Elk, which were hunted down in the rapids, were attracted by water to the rocky shores, where they made an easy target for hunters.

(1975: 42)

Malmer's comments about elk being attracted to the water appear rather curious considering the widespread availability of surface water in northern Sweden. Hagen (1976: 35–9 and 128–9) also refers to the rapids as an animal trap, while stating that there must have been an intimate connection between the carvings and hunting beliefs (referring to Figure 31 as depicting a collective hunting scene) but provides no further specific suggestions.

Baudou (1977: 82) argues that there is no necessary correlation between the hunting and depiction of elks. Pointing to the absence of elk bones at the settlement site, he argues that Nämforsen was not an elk trap but a seasonally occupied summer salmon fishing site at which hunting tools were also fabricated for use elsewhere. This would also correlate with seasonal availability of the rocks for carving during snow- and ice-free periods. On account of the large size of the settlement site Baudou also remarks that Nämforsen may have been a major ritual centre. Ramqvist, Forsberg and Backe (1985), in their report on the recently discovered carving site at Stornorrfors (see Table 11 and Figure 21), continue this line of argument and insert Nämforsen into what is claimed to be a 'predictive model'. They note that during the time in which the carvings were produced both Stornorrfors and Nämforsen were situated at the lowest-lying major rapids on their respective river courses and as such were important summer salmon fishing locations. Other carving sites yet to be found might therefore also be located at similar locations according to regional land upheaval curves, on other rivers in northern Sweden. According to them, elks might be considered to be a 'critical resource' during the winter months. Because of this economic role elks were depicted in large numbers even when they were not actually being hunted.

In addition to these simple arguments linking the depiction of elks to their dietary importance and the site of Nämforsen to elk trapping or summer fishing or ritual, trade or exchange has also been suggested. Hallström (1960: 373) and Malmer (1975: 44–5) both note the position of Nämforsen very near to a bay of the sea and suggest that this was a site at which exchange of furs and hides and other goods took place with 'southern merchants', hence a southern Bronze Age 'influence' on motif form, in particular on the boats. Malmer notes that in the absence of any exploitable resources of copper or tin in Scandinavia 'the greatest importation of bronze from continental Europe to south Scandinavia had to be paid for in some way, and furs were a more probable payment than the products of south Scandinavian farming' (1976: 45). Furthermore, this metal (at least to Sweden and Norway) must have arrived by boat. He makes the further interesting comment that 'the fact that the profits from this trade, the bronzes, remained in areas with a strong economy – Denmark and Scania – is not exceptional in economic history: indeed it is typical' (Malmer 1981: 107; see also the discussion below, pp. 158–64).

While elks, then, were supposedly being depicted because of their dietary significance, and as a totemic symbol, boats were presumably carved as a result of, or to indicate the importance of, exchange. This hotch-potch of explanations hardly does justice to the form and complexity of the carvings at Nämforsen. What all these explanations have in common is their failure to deal with the specificity and complexity of the carved rock surfaces. There is no consideration of why we find various motif combinations on different carved rock surfaces. All that is purported to be explained is why elks or boats occur at all at Nämforsen rather than, say, wombats or spacecraft. The rock carvings themselves actively resist such explanations for the simple reason that they are virtually ignored in the accounts. No specific explanation is given for the presence of fish, birds, shoe soles, tools or humans, or indeed the depiction of different types of boats.

The strongest case is for hunting magic and a functionalist account of elk totemism. The factors in favour of this idea are:

1 The undoubted economic significance of the elk, which we know about from the large numbers of elk bones from settlement sites.
2 The preponderance of elk depictions. This would fit well in terms of a thesis suggesting it was the act of carving the elk that was of vital significance rather than the representation itself. However, such an argument runs into difficulties in accounting for the wide variety in the forms of the elk depictions and in the fact that, while some are executed in a very naturalistic or realistic manner, others appear rather clumsy. This might, of course, be explained away in terms of the competence of individual artisans.
3 The widespread use of elk symbolism. Elk heads occur on poles, in some cases held upright by phallic men, and on the prows of boats. People are shown in close juxtaposition to elks, in some cases combined with them to form mythological beings.

Against such a functionalist interpretation it may be noted that (a) there is only one certain case of an elk depiction pierced by a projectile; (b) there are no depictions of anything resembling an elk trap; (c) only a few cases of elks might be reasonably interpreted as pregnant females; (d) there is an almost complete absence of depictions of primary sexual organs for the elks or secondary sexual characteristics such as the presence of antlers; (e) there is an absence of animal copulation scenes and only one involving humans. The carvings do not then seem to be primarily about hunting activities or increasing elk fertility. Beyond all this there is the problem of how to relate the elks to the other depictions at Nämforsen. It would be fairly easy to extend the hypothesis that elks were being portrayed because of their dietary significance to two other classes of representations: the fish and the birds. These were also carved because they were good to eat. Yet it is quite clear that Nämforsen does not simply represent a prehistoric menu. Shoe soles and boats are hardly edible; and the beaver, which we know from the settlement evidence to be, if anything, a more important economic resource than either birds or fish, is absent, as are other potential game animals.

What we need to explain is why it is only elks, fish and birds that occur at Nämforsen and no functionalist thesis can help us here. We also need to explain why there are tools, shoe soles, humans and boats; why certain combinations of these designs are permissible on

individual carving surfaces and others not. There is little doubt that
(a) elk did constitute a very important economic resource; (b)
Nämforsen was an important salmon fishing location; (c) Nämforsen
constituted a ritual centre and (d) it may also have featured in an
extensive exchange network between southern and northern Sweden.
These observations, all of which are important, need to be taken
much further through detailed consideration of the carved rock
surfaces themselves if we are to understand further the meaning of
the de*signs* and their relationships.

The complexity of the rock carving surfaces actively resist
functional explanations for the simple reason that virtually nothing
is in fact explained. The functionalist theories purporting to explain
Nämforsen do not explain the empirical phenomena in a manner
that avoids arbitrariness. They in no way provide an adequate
understanding of the content of the rock carvings and their form.
The detail of the rock carvings is either left unaccounted for or
considered merely contingent or arbitrary. It is clear that tying the
carvings down to the 'realistic' and considering that the de*sign*
signifies only itself does not take us very far. The problem has been
to concentrate attention on the de*signs* themselves rather than the
relations between them. It is the relations that perhaps provide the
meaning, not the things in themselves. The functionalist arguments
obviously get us nowhere in terms of 'why' questions (why these
particular de*signs*; why these particular de*sign* relationships); however, they do obviously have some relevance in terms of 'where'
questions in relation to site location, i.e. the exploitation of salmon
runs, the possible importance of coastal contacts and the role
Nämforsen may have played as a central ritual aggregation site. It is
therefore not a question of rejecting all functionalist arguments
outright but realizing their severe limitations. Hunting magic
theories can be rejected outright along with totemic functionalism
but there still seems to be great utility in a totemic structuralist
thesis (see below).

RELATIONALITY AND MEANING

I have already stressed the relational significance of the designs and
the fact that only a limited number of combinational possibilities is
being used on individual rock carving surfaces. De*sign* combination
is not a random process but structured according to a definite set of
rules (Tables 2–5). One way in which the question of signification

53

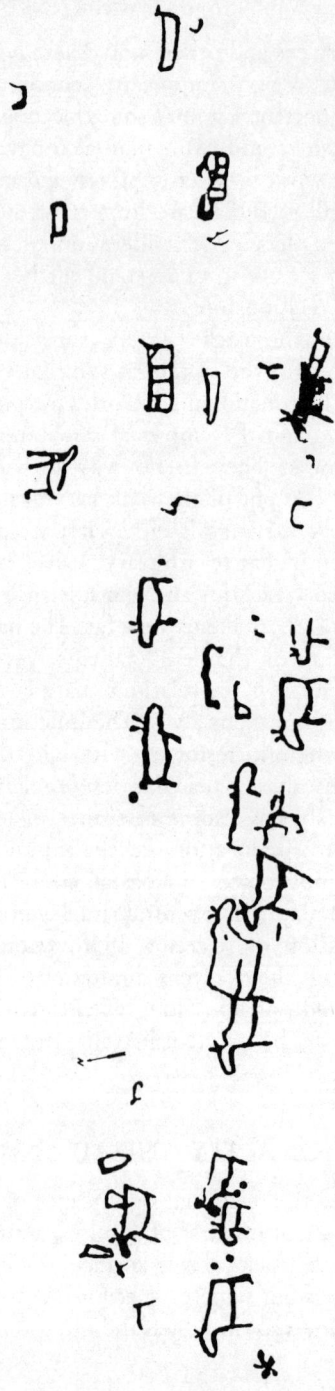

Figure 23 Rock carving surface on Notön (Location: Figure 16, No. 1. Source: Hallström 1960: Plate XVI: C:3. Scale: 1:20).

This carving surface depicts at least fourteen elks and six boats. All the certain boats are grouped to the right, the elks to the left. Most of the elks are grouped in twos or threes. Only one pair directly confront one another. An unusual three-legged elk is 'upside down'. Two elks are partially conjoined and there is only one case involving a significant degree of overlap. This is between the only elk depicted in scooped as opposed to outline technique and a double-lined boat. This carving surface is a simple display of the two chief representational designs at Nämforsen. The scooped elk stands out from all the others and serves to emphasize an intimate connection between elks and boats yet at the same time the spatial separation between elks to the left and boats to the right indicates that this is an oppositional relationship. It is at precisely the point that the elk group terminates and the boat group begins that the overlap takes place.

Figure 24 Rock carving surface, northern river banks (Location: Figure 13, No. 1. Source: Hallström 1960: Plate X: A:9. Scale 1: 20).

A more or less diagonal linear series consisting of eight to nine elks and four boats, one of which is single lined. There is no overlap on this carving surface and it appears to be simply a relational display of elements. Again it is the intimate connection between elks and boats that is being emphasized. The only two motifs to fuse together are a small elk and double-line boat more or less at the centre of the carving. The elk–boat association is further emphasized by the opposition between the largest elk (in scooped technique) and the largest boat, which is also the only boat to possess internal hull division. On its prow peculiar trailing 'ears' appear.

---

can be taken further is to consider those de*signs* which are super-positioned. There is no shortage of surfaces for rock carving at Nämforsen and, indeed, what appear to be rather rough surfaces were sometimes chosen in preference to smoother, more glossy rocks. Furthermore, in many instances some of the rock surfaces that were carved are either just above the waterline or in some cases were on rocks that can only have been exposed during periods of very low water. For much of the year some of the carvings must have been covered by the swirling river waters. The difficulty and danger of actually reaching the islands in the river channel needs to be remembered as well as the precipitous nature of some of the rocks. In view of all this, cases of de*sign* overlap are of particular interest. Such overlap must have been intentional. The occurrence of overlapping different de*sign* classes is not very common when compared with overlapping between de*signs* of the same class, e.g.

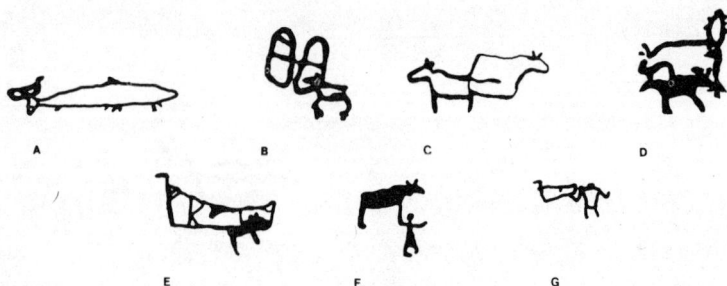

Figure 25 Some examples of de*sign* superpositioning and merging taken from different rock carving surfaces at Nämforsen. A: boat + fish; B: shoe sole + elk; C: elk + elk; D: scooped elk + outline elk + fish; E: boat + elk; F: elk + stick-line human; G: boat + 'triangular' or outline human

when an elk is partially or completely transposed over another elk. In all there are about fifty clearly identifiable cases (Table 6). By far the most common cases of overlap are between elks and boats and elks and humans. Elks overlap with every other de*sign* class except tools. Overlap between other classes of de*sign* is confined to one or two examples. This suggests, first, a special and important set of relations between elks, boats and humans and, second, the elk as the only de*sign* class that links together all the others. We may distinguish between these cases of de*sign* overlap (Figure 25) and situations in which one de*sign* merges or joins another at distal points or in a more obviously intentional way. Here I refer to the presence of human figures in boats or people holding tools or elks conjoined to the ends of boats. Since we know that there is a special relationship between elks, boats and humans, it is appropriate at this stage to consider each of these de*sign* classes in more detail.

Table 7 The presence of overlapping between different de*sign* classes according to topographical pages of the text

Design *overlap*	*Page I*	*Page II*	*Page III*	*Page IV*
elk + boat	+	−	+	+
elk + fish	+	−	−	−
boat + fish	−	+	−	−
elk + human	+	−	+	+
elk + tool	−	−	+	−
boat + human	−	−	−	+
boat + bird	−	−	−	+
elk + shoe sole	−	−	+	−

5

DESIGN FORM

THE DE*SIGN* OF THE ELK

I have noted that elks constitute by far the most common de*sign* class at Nämforsen (55 per cent of the de*signs*). They overlap and/or merge with every other de*sign* class. A clear binary division exists in the manner in which elks are depicted. They either have bodies executed in outline or as scooped forms in which the entire body is pecked out on the rock surface. The latter make up around 55 per cent of the total number of elks. Outline and scooped forms occur together on only twenty-nine carving surfaces (18 per cent of the total number on which elks appear). In those cases where the two forms of elk do occur together on the same carving surface, they are in most cases spatially separated in different areas and one of the two forms always predominates, i.e. many scooped forms are 'offset' by a few outline elks or vice versa.

Some other features of interest may now be discussed. In six cases elks have double heads, one at either end of the body, and this seems to be of particular importance in view of the large numbers of elks that lack heads altogether (Table 8; Figure 27). This figure would appear to be too high to be explained as entirely the result of differential preservation. What we may be witnessing is not the depiction of elks *as* elks but as a series of body parts which in many cases may coalesce in the form of a single animal but need not necessarily do so.

Now, of course, such statistics might be automatically rejected as being solely due to problems of preservation. This is the most obvious 'explanation' but is inadequate as a total explanation for the entire material in view of other evidence. Not only do some elks lack certain body parts but the depiction of parts of the body varies

Figure 26 Rock carving surface, Brådön (Location: Figure 15, No. 3. Source: Hallström 1960: Plate XXIV: E:2–3. Scale: 1:20).

Here there are at least twelve elks, one fish (salmon) and three pairs of shoe soles. The large central elk is the biggest one to appear on any carving surface at Nämforsen being 1.14 m in length. The other carvings appear puny in comparison. There is a considerable degree of overlap both between the elks (one of which is entirely scooped out) and in the superpositioning of the fish and one elk in outline technique. The shoe soles do not overlap with any other design form. Some of the elks appear to be in movement but movement or its absence is not significant in this context. The huge elk naturalistically displayed with cloven hooves and chin tuft is of great significance. A very simple and effective way to emphasize import-ance is, of course, to stress size and dimensionality.

This carving surface displays various elements – elks, fish, shoe soles – and establishes a connection between them, emphasizing the most important element of all, the elk. It appears therefore to be highly significant that this rock carving surface should be situated at the centre of the Nämforsen rock carving area and on the same rock as the one with the circle cross (see Figures 19 and 15).

Figure 27 Examples of headless and double-headed elks taken from different carving surfaces at Nämforsen

Table 8 The absence of various body parts in elk depictions

No head		Front leg missing		Back leg missing		No legs		Partial depictions	
n	%	n	%	n	%	n	%	n	%
70	10	55	8	76	11	29	4	183	27

in emphasis. There is considerable evidence to suggest that importance was placed on depictions of the front or back legs and that this bears some relation to the presence or absence of front or back legs. By differential emphasis on front or back legs I refer to thickening, length, angle, provision or non-provision of hooves or 'toes' (Figure 28) in the case of animals with two legs. The front leg is emphasized in 160 cases (28 per cent of animals with two legs) and the back leg in 198 cases (35 per cent). If we consider all the cases of animals (i) without a front or back leg or (ii) without any legs at all or (iii) with two legs but with differential emphasis on the front or the back leg the total number is 431 or 64 per cent.

We can examine the depictions of elks with regard to whether they appear to be static, lifeless representations with straight, stiff legs, or indicate movement (Figure 30). The former type dominate

Figure 28 Elks: examples of front/back leg differentiation taken from different carving surfaces at Nämforsen

Figure 29 Rock carving surface, Brådön (Location: Figure 15, No. 4. Source: Hallström 1960: Plate XXIV: D:2. Scale: 1:20).

The surface consists of four outline elks and one shoe sole placed roughly in the middle. The elks are clearly paired: two confront each other while the other pair are placed back to back. The elks to the left appear entirely static (cf. Figure 19); those to the right with their bending legs appear to be moving. It might be suggested that the de*sign* of the shoe sole asserts influence and has definite effects in relation to the form of the elk.

Figure 30 Examples of passive and active elks taken from different carving surfaces at Nämforsen

while frequencies of active animals vary considerably between the main topographical carving pages (Table 9).

Table 9 Relative frequencies of active elks according to main topographically defined carving page

Page I	Page II	Page III	Page IV
29	41	60	19

These figures have considerable interest in relation to depictions of humanity. Where human depictions are absent (page II) or comparatively infrequent (page III: see Table 1), frequencies of active elks are much higher and this can be seen clearly by comparing the elks on the major carving surface on Brådön with those on Notön (Figures 19 and 33). Part of the meaning and significance of some carving surfaces may be to do with control over elks. It is of interest to note that, of those elks which can possibly be identified as possessing antlers, all of these with one exception are executed in outline form. There are no clear relationships between outline and scooped forms according to whether they face right or left, are depicted as active or passive, or in terms of the absence of specific body parts.

Some other interesting features may now be noted. Virtually all of the boats are provided with elk heads on their prows in either a naturalistic or a simplified form (see Figure 39). Second, in a number of cases elks and humans actually merge into 'mythical' beings (Figures 9 and 31). Third, in other cases, elks merge with boats or are placed in a direct and oppositional relationship with them (Figures 23, 38, 43, 45). Fourth, there is the class of clearly ceremonial objects or tools possessing a straight or curved handle terminated by an elk head with ears. Hallström refers to these as 'elk-head axes' (Figure 32). There are about twenty examples in the topographically defined carving pages I, III and IV, either as isolated motifs or on decks of ships or held by human bodies. Hallström points out similarities between these depictions and sculpted stone elk heads of approximately the same date occurring in settlement sites from the late Neolithic of northern Sweden.

Figure 31　Examples of merging elk–humans and elk–human super-positioning taken from different carving surfaces at Nämforsen

Figure 32　Examples of elk heads on poles occurring on decks of single-line boats and as independent de*signs* taken from different carving surfaces at Nämforsen

Elks are depicted in only two or three cases with four legs. In all other instances they are shown in a heavily stylized manner, in profile, with only one front and/or back leg. As already mentioned, they occur in great numbers and on 161 or 70 per cent of the individual carving surfaces. Numbers on carving surfaces vary considerably (Table 10).

Table 10 The frequency of elks on individual carving surfaces with different de*sign* relationships. Examples: on forty-six carving surfaces only one isolated elk is portrayed while on five carving surfaces on which only elks and boats occur two elks are depicted.

Frequency of carving surfaces with:	Frequency of elks									
	1	2	3	4	5	6	7–12	13–20	21–40	>40
elks only	46	17	4	1	4	2	5	–	–	–
elks + boats	7	5	3	2	–	2	3	1	–	–
elks + humans	2	–	1	1	1	2	2	–	–	–
elks + footsole	1	–	–	–	–	–	–	–	–	–
elk + boat + tool	2	1	2	1	–	1	–	–	–	–
elk + boat + human	3	–	–	–	–	–	–	–	–	1
elk + fish + human	–	–	–	–	–	–	–	–	1	–
elk + boat + human + tool	–	–	1	–	–	–	2	–	1	–
elk + boat + bird + footsole	–	1	–	–	–	–	–	–	–	–
elk + boat + human + tool + bird + fish	–	–	–	–	–	–	–	–	–	1
all designs	–	–	–	–	–	–	–	–	–	1

From Table 10 it is apparent that elks occur in great numbers only when depicted on a carving surface with humans and other design forms, principally boats. Where elks occur alone, they are in small numbers. There are only five carving surfaces on which more than six elks are depicted. The maximum number is eleven. Where elks occur solely with humans they are portrayed in frequencies ranging between one and seven, in one case eleven.

We know from modern ethological studies of hunted elk populations

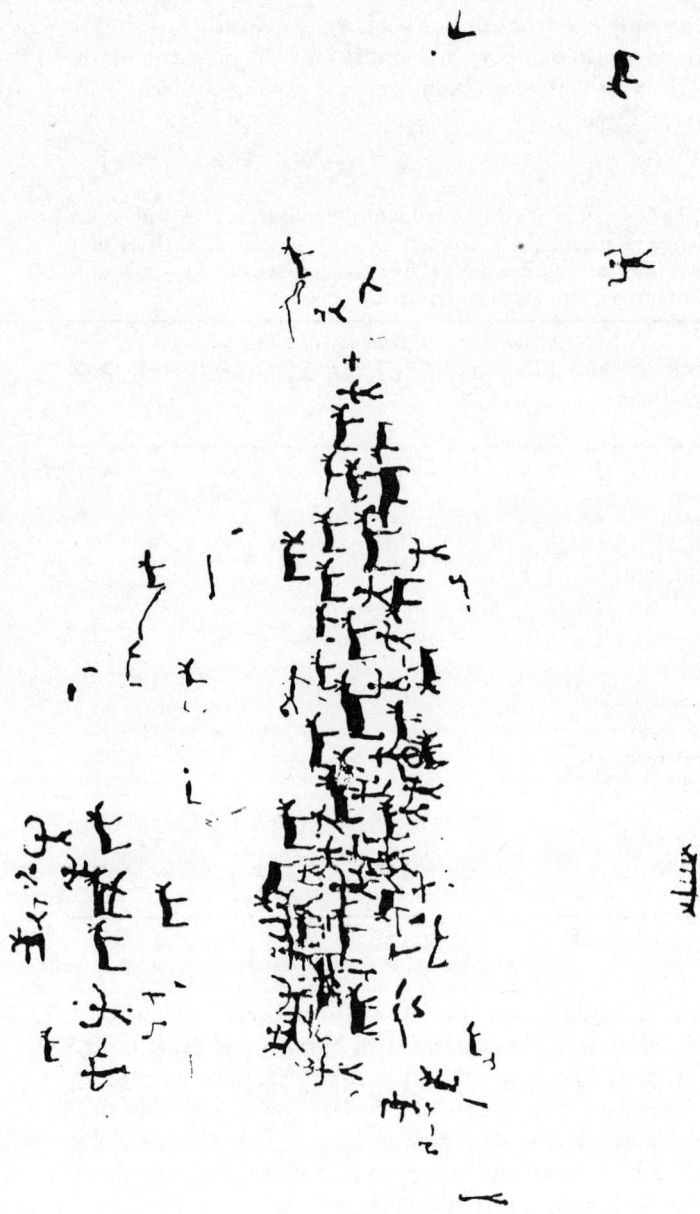

Figure 33 Rock carving surface, Notön (Location: Figure 16, No. 2. Source: Hallström 1960: Plate XX: Q1. Scale: 1:20).

About forty-two elks, thirty stick-line humans and two single-line boats, and an elk head on a pole, comprise this large carving surface. All the figures with the exception of one outline elk, in a marginal position to the right of the main body of carvings, are executed by scooping away the rock surface. What is of importance here is the elk–human relationship. It is perhaps not surprising, then, that the boats should appear as both isolated and in marginal positions.

Hallström (1960: 234) attempts to explain the isolation of the boats by suggesting that the lower part of the carving surface (equally good for carving as the upper part) may have been periodically blocked with boulders carried by the river current and thus not available for use apart from small gaps on which the boats were depicted. Such an explanation does not seem very convincing in that (a) it is boats that are placed here rather than humans or elks; (b) since so much trouble was expended on the carvings one might expect that shifting a few boulders if necessary would hardly be beyond the bounds of human possibility; (c) throughout the Nämforsen area some carving surfaces are utilized while others equally good are ignored; (d) Hallström's 'explanation' seems to suggest that – here at least – if a rock surface for carving was available it would have both been utilized and more or less continuously filled with motifs.

This is the only carving surface at Nämforsen on which large numbers of humans occur. Indeed no less than one-third of all human depictions are found here. The elk–human ratio is roughly 1.5: 1.0 whereas in most cases on carving surfaces on which both elks and humans occur it can be anything up to 25:1. The elks are depicted in a stiff, rigid, one might almost say 'domesticated', posture. The only elk that appears to be moving stands out in that it possesses four legs – one of the very few four-legged animal depictions at Nämforsen. All the elks apart from three at the extreme left and 'top' of the carving surface are orientated west–east. They are densely crowded, interspersed and surrounded by human depictions. At least four of the human bodies are clearly phallic. One rather indistinct human figure, more or less at the centre of the main mass of figures, carries an elk head on a pole. An isolated elk head on a pole occurs to the left. Despite the clustering of the elks there appears to be a degree of linearity in the depictions (found also on many other carving surfaces at Nämforsen, cf. Figure 17 above). In the larger group most elks face right or east in two parallel rows. The elks facing left or west are at the bottom with one isolated example at the top left of the main group. In connection with those elks orientated north–south this seems to suggest a circular dispersion: as if the elks are being rounded up. This impression gains stronger force from the numerous instances of human figures with upraised arms, especially in view of the fact that figures with upraised arms are sometimes outside the rows of elks. This is particularly clear in the smaller northernmost mass of elk and human figures. Furthermore, while the elks appear to be static, many of the humans are in vigorous movement.

that elk or moose are not herd animals. Elk are primarily browsers of deciduous shrubs and trees and there is a strong relationship between the quantity and quality of such vegetation and elk density (Ahlén 1975). Elk are generally more dispersed and mobile during snow-free seasons. Average annual elk density in northern Sweden in the 1940s ranged between 3.9 and 19.0/1,000 ha (Petersen 1955: 204–5) and more recent statistics fall within this range. Forsberg (1985: 20) cites various figures from northern Sweden and the taiga belt of Russia in the range of 0.4–5.0 elks/sq. km. In general elk density in northern Sweden decreases from south to north and from coastal areas in the east to the mountain foothills in the west.

Peterson (1955: 107) notes that a gregarious instinct is less developed in the elk or moose than in any other North American hoofed wild mammal and the same observation is also true for northern Europe. The only well-developed social instincts are mother–young relationships and sometimes yearling relationships amongst offspring. Elk are either solitary most of the year or are found in groups of two or three (Mochi and Carter 1971: 64). Sometimes in winter, if there is deep snow, larger numbers of elk may 'yard up' together, usually between three and five animals, although on rare occasions as many as fifteen to twenty have been reported (Peterson 1955: 107). The only other time in which elks appear in large numbers is during seasonal upland–lowland migrations. Such migrations occur on a limited scale in northern Sweden.

The massive aggregations of elks seen at Nämforsen on some carving surfaces may perhaps represent migrating elks; they are frequently depicted in rows or columns (Figure 33) but there are two other obvious possibilities: (1) Human interference has altered elk behaviour patterns drastically and in the past they might have aggregated in much larger numbers. On ecological and ethological grounds this seems very unlikely. (2) The depiction of elks is not at all a display of reality but a cosmological view of the world. On the one hand the presence of double-headed, headless, and elk–human, elk–boat and elk-head pole depictions give strong grounds for questioning the validity of these being simply depictions of ecological 'reality'. On the other hand it would be unwise to set up an artificial either/or dichotomy: the carving surfaces accurately depict socioeconomic realities or they have nothing to do with them. It is interesting to note that the carvings at Nämforsen are of an entirely different nature from informational depictions with regard to hunting practices and game movements etc. For example, Jochelson (1926) gives examples of picture drawings from Siberian Tungus populations that do have an obvious economic significance, showing routes, good fishing spots, game movements, etc. in relation to the landscape. These picture drawings provide a total contrast with the depictions at Nämforsen, which have no apparent practical value.

It seems most fruitful to regard cosmology as mapping onto features of the natural world and these features, in turn, being incorporated in cosmological systems. Religion becomes the economy and the economy becomes religion and neither can be separated out from the other. Taking up this position we avoid a layer-cake (infrastructure–superstructure) model of the social totality in which the latter is read off from the former, as in the work of Lewis-Williams (1982) on southern African rock art, in which the simple claim is made that the infrastructure or economic base (conceived by him in terms of social relations of production as dominant), is 'the key to understanding ideology' (Lewis-Williams 1982: 431).

In this respect it is interesting to note that in the spring of 1988 an exceptionally large migration of thirty-six elks was sighted and photographed in northern Sweden (*Arbetet*: 20 April 1988). The animals formed a slow-moving column one behind the other. It is such columns of elks that are depicted on some of the carving surfaces at Nämforsen (see e.g. Figures 17 and 33). Such an observation, however, hardly copes with an understanding of the great variability in the depictions of elk and the relationship between elk de*signs* and others. In a somewhat analogous manner, but now shifting from the ecological to the social, Lewis-Williams' excellent discussion of trance states among !Kung shaman expressed in some rock paintings does not exhaust the detail and specificity of the material he analyses. He is prevented from going further by insufficient attention to relationships between designs. Ignoring form, he concentrates almost exclusively on putative meaning content as a direct reflection of social relations of production.

Only mature male elks possess antlers growing from September until December, with shedding taking place in the late autumn. At Nämforsen almost all the elks (with the exception of seven possible cases) possess ears but lack horns. Those elks with horns or antlers occur in three cases on rock surfaces in close association with humans and/or boats, in three others only with hornless elks, and

Figure 34 Rock carving surface, northern river banks (Location: Figure 13, No. 2. Source: Hallström 1960: Plate XIV: F:1. Scale: 1:20) Note ambiguous elk antler/single-line boat association. Examples of single-line boats taken from other carving surfaces at Nämforsen are shown to the right.

here the form of the antlers is different. In the first set of cases the antlers appear ambiguously like single-line boats, in the second they appear like extended ears. So it may be the case that these depictions are not of antlers at all, even here, but an intimate and deliberately ambiguous elk–boat association on the one hand and extended ears on the other (Figure 34). The possible presence of antlers on one elk cannot be explained in this manner but this elk has other unusual features. It is one of only three elks at Nämforsen to possess three legs.

Now, the lack of horns or antlers suggests strongly that it is only female elks that are being depicted. This point has been considered by others. Hagen (1976: 63) and Mikkelsen (1986: 140) suggest that it may be an indication that the rock carvings were created during the winter and/or represent a preference for hunting elks during the winter. Ramqvist, Forsberg and Backe (1985: 355) likewise suggest that it is elks in their winter state that are being portrayed. Hallström (1960: 290) argues that the ears were a good substitute for the antlers on account of the technical difficulty of depicting the latter. However, according to this line of argument all the elks would then presumably be male! If the *design* of the elk does not simply mean elk but something other, then the ambiguity encountered in the sexual determination of the elks would seem to be highly important.

INSUFFICIENT BODIES

Human figures appear on thirty-one carving surfaces (13 per cent). In total there are ninety-two identifiable individual bodies (8 per cent of the total designs at Nämforsen) (Table 1). I have already noted the absence of human bodies as isolated depictions on individual carving surfaces. They always occur in association with other design classes. Cases of actual conjunction between human bodies and elk bodies have also been mentioned. In others, bodies appear on ships (eight separate vessels with between one and seven clearly distinguishable bodies as opposed to so-called 'crew strokes'). So there is an intimate association between humans, elks and boats.

Figure 35 Depictions of humans: examples of stick-line bodies carrying poles, elk heads on poles and tools and triangular bodies taken from different carving surfaces at Nämforsen

A number hold tools or implements: elk heads on poles. This is of particular interest in view of the widespread distribution of sculpted figurines, daggers and ornaments with elk heads in northern Sweden, Finland and western Siberia from the Mesolithic, Neolithic and Bronze Age and the occurrence of carved horn elk heads on poles in graves from western Siberia (Hallström 1960: 365; Carpelan 1975; Lindqvist 1978). The humans also hold in four, possibly five, cases poles with a rounded or extended base, angular implements in six cases and possibly spears or hunting weapons in two or three cases (Figure 35). The rest of the figures (*c.* seventy) are neither armed nor carrying weapons or implements of any kind.

Figure 36 Rock carving surface, northern river banks (Location: Figure 13, No. 3. Source: Hallström 1960: Plate XIV: F:2. Scale: 1: 20).

This is the only carving surface at Nämforsen on which the number of human bodies is numerically greater than those of elk depictions. Four humans and three elks can be clearly identified. It is consequently of great interest that this is also the only carving surface on which a love scene is depicted 'overlooked' (in the context of Nämforsen I feel inclined to say 'of course') by an elk. To the right a third human body with a distinct thickening around the middle indicating perhaps a pregnant woman is associated with a further two elks. A fourth human figure stands behind the elk overlooking the love scene.

As with the elks, sexual determination is ambiguous. Bodies with clear phalluses are limited in number. In two cases the men hold an elk head on a pole; in a third case there is a direct association with a two-headed elk; in another an isolated phallic man stands amidst elks. There appears to be a strong association between men and tools and elks in a variety of ways. Two figures with a thickening around the stomach may indicate pregnant women. It is significant that these are the only cases in which women can possibly be identified (Figures 7 and 36). We might imagine that, if it was important to represent females and female reproductive capacities, this would not have been beyond the technical possibilities of rock engraving – breasts, for example, could be depicted, or sexual organs.

It is interesting to note that there is overwhelming evidence to suggest that humans are not being depicted in normal labouring activities. In only one or two cases does a body hold an implement that might have been at all useful in hunting or fishing or gathering. Furthermore, it has already been noted that there is only one clear

Figure 37 Rock carving surface, Notön (Location: Figure 13, No. 3. Source: Hallström 1960: Plate XIV: U:1. Scale: 1: 20).

This carving surface displays depictions of two humans with outline or 'triangular' bodies, nine boats, two birds, one fish and two angular implements or tools. The fish appears to be harpooned while one human body holds an enormous scythe-like object and another a double-lined boat with appended animal (elk) head. The body holding the scythe is the only human executed in outline style which might be considered to be phallic but this detail is uncertain. This carving surface, in common with all the others at Nämforsen, is scaleless. The scale adopted is not that of a Euclidean measured space. The fish and the angular tools are enormous in comparison with the boats, as indeed are the human figures. The upper carving group appears to be arranged in a staggered linear series contrasting with the human, boat and tool depictions below. As on other carving surfaces at Nämforsen, there is an obvious similarity in depictions of birds and boats yet this is somewhat compensated for by only the former appearing in scooped technique. With elks absent, the key relational element on this carving surface is the boats: in the upper group associated with birds and fish, in the lower with humanity. There is no significant degree of overlap between different motif forms.

case of an elk with an arrow lodged in its body. The implements held or portrayed as individual depictions are ceremonial in nature. There are also other obvious absences: huts, domestic scenes, clothing, everyday utensils. As Helskog has noted for the site of Alta (1987), there is an outside rather than an inside art, emphasizing the public rather than the private.

The posture of the human depictions is stereotyped and stiff in many cases: full face, legs apart and arms hanging down or stretched upwards in twenty cases. The stereotyped and lifeless posture of some of the humans finds its counterpart in that of the majority of

Figure 38 Rock carving surface, Notön (Location: Figure 13, No. 4. Source: Hallström 1960: Plate XVI: A:2. Scale: 1:20).

Three, possibly four elks, three human bodies, two or more tools and six boats are combined on this carving surface. Only one boat is depicted by a scooped technique; the rest of the figures are outline double-lined vessels. The elks are portrayed in a static pose, the uppermost one with conjoined legs. Humanity appears in a marginal position. One body rises up from a large, double-lined boat with simplified elk-head prow and 'crew strokes'. Two other bodies 'float' to the top left. The two centrally positioned elks face one another. The elk to the right is conjoined with a tangled mass of lines depicting two double-lined boats and fragments of a fourth elk. At the bottom two double-lined boats are linked and the largest boat merges with the rear of an elk. Both this boat and the elk face in the same direction: right or east.

the elks. The human depictions fall into two distinctive categories: stick-line figures and those with 'triangular' bodies. The stick-line figures occur on carving pages I, III and IV while those with triangular bodies are confined to Notön (page IV), with only one exception which occurs on what has already been suggested to be the central carving surface on Brådön (Figure 19). The triangular figures are comparatively few in number (twelve cases) and they are all in intimate association with double-line boats. They never appear on carving surfaces on which single-line boats are depicted.

THE DESIGN OF THE BOAT

One of the features of the Nämforsen rock carvings which has been stressed over and over again is their inherent ambiguity – their openness to alternative interpretations, meanings and associations. Boat depictions are by far the most variable at Nämforsen. In this they differ markedly from the fairly standardized depictions of elks or humans (or even more from fish or shoe soles). Figure 39 attempts to capture some of the extant variety and Table 11 presents some of the results of an analysis.

Table 11 Frequencies of boat types by topographical carving page. Code numbers refer to Figure 39.

Code	Page I		Page II		Page III		Page IV		Total (all pages)	
	n	%	n	%	n	%	n	%	n	%
1	19	7	43	16	28	10	183	67	273	86
2	19	46	1	2	6	15	15	36	41	12
3	–	–	–	–	–	–	6	100	6	2
11	5	6	9	10	12	14	61	70	87	28
12	13	7	34	19	14	8	118	66	179	56
111	1	4	2	9	5	23	14	64	22	7
112	3	7	5	12	3	7	34	75	45	14
113	–	–	–	–	–	–	2	100	2	0.6
114	–	–	–	–	–	–	6	100	6	2
121	4	10	5	12	4	10	27	67	40	12
122	5	6	15	18	7	8	57	68	84	26
123	–	–	–	–	–	–	4	100	4	1
124	2	16	2	16	3	25	5	41	12	3

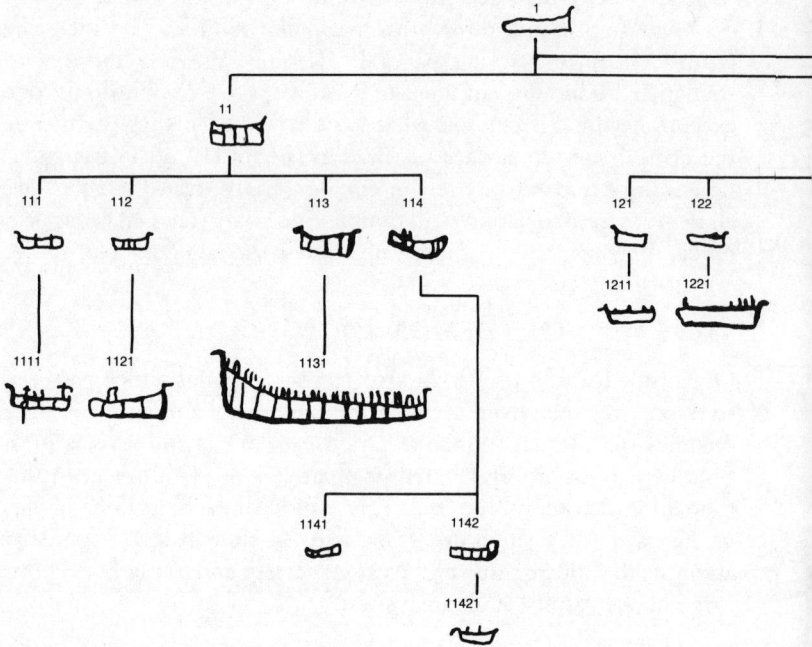

Figure 39 A hierarchical classification system for boat forms at Nämforsen. Scale of the de*signs* 1: 20. Explanation of coding system: 1: double-line boats; 2: single-line boats; 3: scooped boats; 11: double-line boats with internal hull division (ribs); 12: without ribs. Each of these forms is then subdivided according to whether the prow with simplified animal (elk) head faces left (111, 121), right (112, 122), possesses two heads at either end (113, 123) or no heads (114, 124). At the next level boats are subdivided according to whether 'crew strokes' and/or people are depicted as deck figures (1111, 1121, 1131, 1211, 1221, 1231). Boats lacking appended animal heads are subdivided according to presence/absence of 'crew strokes'/people (11421, 12421). Single-line boats are subdivided according to whether elk head faces left (21) or right (22) or is appended at both ends (23) or is absent (24). Scooped forms are too infrequent to be subdivided.

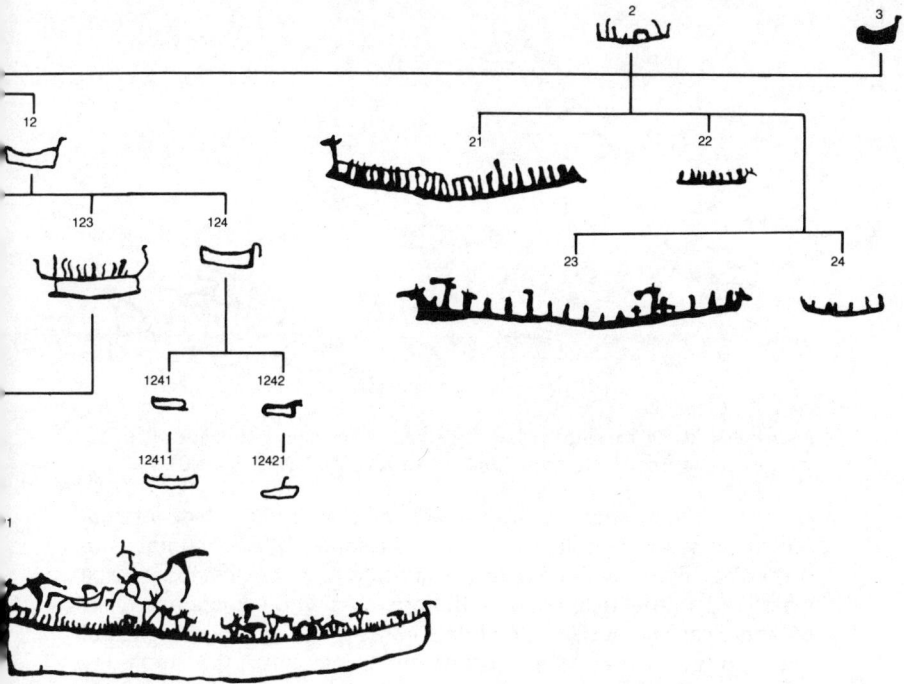

Of the three basic boat forms distinguished in Figure 39, double-lined boats dominate in all carving pages except page I. Scooped forms are confined to page IV where, as we might expect, the greatest variability in boat form occurs. Single-lined forms are most frequent on page I while virtually absent on page II. Double-lined forms lacking internal hull division are twice as frequent as those with hull division and dominate on pages I, II and IV, while on page III there are roughly equal numbers of boats with and without hull division. A very high proportion (*c.* 80 per cent) of boats have simplified animals but by far the most striking and obvious animal heads appear on large, single-lined vessels. Double-lined boats with animal heads at both ends are found in only a few cases on page IV while single-lined boats with animal heads at prow and stern are more widespread, occurring on pages I, III and IV.

Double-lined boats, irrespective of whether they possess or do not possess internal hull division, more frequently have their prows facing right on page IV while double-lined forms without hull division face predominantly right on page II. On the other pages, numbers of left- or right-facing double-lined boat forms are

Figure 40 Rock carving surface, southern river banks (Location: Figure 14, No. 1. Source: Hallström 1960: Plate XV: Z: 2. Scale: 1: 20).

At least sixteen small, double-lined boats, one with clear internal hull division and one elk, all carved in the same outline technique are displayed. Four of the boats are 'upside-down'. Most possess a simplified animal (elk) head on the prow. As with depictions of elks on some carving surfaces the boats here appear in subgroupings of between four to five as if in small 'herds'. However, the ambiguity goes much further than this. Many of the boat depictions resemble water birds (e.g. the boat above the largest vessel with internal hull division to the extreme right). Furthermore, the solitary elk fits perfectly into the scene and does not appear to be at all out of place. The removal of the legs would quite easily result in its transformation into the form of a boat.

---

approximately equal. 'Crew strokes' and/or people are not frequent on double-lined boats but are almost always found on single-line boats.

If we consider the carving surfaces on which only boats occur, the three basic forms exhibit clear spatial separation and differing degrees of relationality or association with other motif categories. Double-line boats occur on their own on forty-four carving surfaces, single-line boats on only four, while scooped forms never occur on their own and in only one case just with other (double-line) boats. But the most significant feature is that single- and double-line boats never occur together on the same carving surface except in association with other different motif categories. In addition, this requirement of relationality is clearly greater for the single-line forms, which are rarely depicted on their own.

Boat size varies significantly from small vessels 10 cm in length to large boats up to 2 m. Hallström notes (1960: 294) that there are no details giving any information about how the boats were navigated. For example, there are no depictions of sails, oars or rudders. Furthermore, he points out that the only suitable vessel for use on the river at Nämforsen is a small rowing boat. The larger vessels 'simply do not fit into this narrow woodland valley setting in northern Sweden' (p. 303). Another interesting detail is the actual depiction of the vessels. They are spatially distributed and portrayed on individual carving surfaces in almost exactly the same manner as elks, isolated or in 'herd' type groupings of up to sixteen or more boats. Just as the vast herds of elks depicted did not exist, neither did these large accumulations of small vessels nor the massive ships. What we are dealing with is not reality but a cosmological depiction of it.

To return to the theme of ambiguity, it is interesting to note how similar many of the small, double-lined vessels are to birds or legless elk bodies such that it is difficult to distinguish between them especially when we are dealing with partial representations. Such ambiguity, it might be suggested, is not just the result of incomplete preservation or of a technically inept artisan but is intended to forge connections and links. But what is the meaning?

6

MOBILE SPACE, ARRESTED TIME

The physical location of the carvings at Nämforsen also constitutes part of their meaning and their ambiguity. The site is fluid in both the literal and the metaphorical sense of this word. The relations between land and water, the river and the islands, the rapids and the sea coast, carved rocks that are visible and those that are temporarily invisible, are both static and constantly changing. The site is physically in motion yet at any one moment it appears unchanging. Nämforsen possesses a unique singularity and yet is constantly changing.

Today Nämforsen is some 40 km from the mouth of the Ångerman river and 140 km from the outer sea coast. At the time when the rock carvings were produced the site would have been at the end of a long, narrow and gradually receding inlet of the open sea. The rock carvings extend over a distance of 500 m along the banks of the Ångerman river and, as mentioned, on two central islands (Figure 11). The height of the falls and rapids at Nämforsen was, before the building of a hydroelectric power station, about 17 m. The volume of water flowing down the Ångerman river alters dramatically according to the season. A large part of the islands may be covered and many of the rock carvings submerged when the water is in full flood. The largest carving surfaces along the northern river banks are all found within areas flooded at high water, being periodically submerged or forming small islets or peninsulas in the rapids (Hallström 1960: 142). All the carvings at Nämforsen are visible only at times of exceptionally low water. Many – and this changes according to water levels – are situated at the water's edge, visible at one moment, invisible the next: both present and absent.

That many of the carvings should be endlessly covered and uncovered by water, revealed and obscured, is not just a feature to

78

be explained by their location in the rapids. First, and most obviously, this location was chosen – the carvings could have been situated inland and away from the river or further upstream or downstream in an area of calmer waters. Second, and much more interesting, the further the carvings lie towards the rapids (to the west and south-west, see Figure 11), the lower they are in relation to the water level. As Hallström notes (p. 194), the reverse might have been expected. This generalization applies both to the carvings on the islands and to those on the river banks.

CARVING SURFACES
AND TOPOGRAPHICAL SPACE

In purely quantitative terms there are eighteen major carving surfaces (i.e. surfaces with at least fifteen identifiable motifs) at Nämforsen with frequencies ranging from this lower figure to more than eighty. Originally there must have been considerably more on many of the rock surfaces. They are found on rocks scattered more or less uniformly throughout the four topographically defined carving groups (Figures 11, 13–16). However, there are no clear rank–order–type correlations between motif frequency on carving surfaces and complexity of motif combinations. The same motif form or two different forms (such as elks and boats) may be repeated many times. On the other hand, carving surfaces with quantitatively few motifs may have a high frequency of motif combination, i.e. four or more different motif types: elks, boats, fish, humans, etc. may occur together. Biggest is not therefore necessarily most complex at Nämforsen although all the major carving surfaces, in quantitative terms, do have a minimum of two or more different design combinations, and we have already noted that the carving surface with the most carvings possesses the greatest number of design combinations.

From Tables 2–5 it is apparent that there are major differences between the four topographically defined carving areas. Differences between relative and absolute frequencies of carving surfaces with only one motif or two different motifs are, as we might expect, broadly in accordance with absolute numbers of different types of design for each area (see Table 1). However, differences in motif composition between carved surfaces with combinations of three or more different design forms appear to be strongly localized, if few in number. By contrast, there are no clear spatial relationships between carved surfaces within each topographical group. Different motif forms or motif combinations are fairly evenly distributed throughout each of the carving areas I–IV (Figures 13–16). For example, we do not find situations in which, say, carving surfaces with only elks occur in a delimited area, surfaces with only boats in another, and surfaces with elks and boats in between. Instead, what we find appears to be an ordered dispersion of different motif forms and combinations throughout each carving area. I suggest that the following principles are being used to structure the spatial dispersion of the carving surfaces both within and between the topographical groups:

1 Lay out and display the motif forms according to their relative importance as either (i) isolated elements e.g. a single fish or (ii) groups of the same element (e.g. a number of fish).
2 Pair different elements (e.g. elks and boats), again according to relative importance, and include in this pairing elements that can only occur together with others (e.g. humans and birds).
3 At a number of locations within each carving area combine different pairs and/or single motifs to create different themes and meaning sets.

CARVING TIME

Space may be in movement at Nämforsen, yet the time of the rock carvings does not flow. There are no convincing premises for arranging any of the motif categories in a clear typological or developmental series. Since the retreat of the ice after the last glaciation, land elevation has taken place in northern Sweden. Nämforsen today lies c. 80 m above sea level. According to the regional upheaval curve for northern Ångermanland (Miller and Robertsson 1979) the Nämforsen area was not exposed before c. 3700 BC so that the carvings cannot possibly be earlier than this date and it is generally supposed (e.g. Bakka 1975; Helskog 1985, 1987; Ramqvist, Forsberg and Backe 1985) that the majority of the northern Scandinavian rock carvings were produced at some time in the period 3500–2000 BC. The rock carvings at Nämforsen seem to have been produced over a period of maximal temporal extent of 1,500 years. The length of time over which the carvings were produced and whether it was continuous, taking place year after year or in discontinuous phases, is unknown.

Unfortunately, overlap of motif forms or conjunctions between carved lines at Nämforsen provides no basis for indicating relative age of motif types. Referring to one of the best preserved carving surfaces at Nämforsen, Hallström notes that intersecting lines do not offer any basis for age determination for the figures (1960: 261). Because of the absence of any stratigraphy or closed finds, arguments about the relative age of various depictions have been entirely based on attempts to trace 'stylistic influence' from northern Norwegian rock carvings or those in Russia or southern Scandinavia. Chronological arguments have been based principally upon the use of different carving techniques to execute animal motifs (either by carving out the design in outline form or scooping out the entire design) and on the basis of boat design form.

Hallström (1960: 286–8) suggests that scooped-out animal figures are a late innovation in north Scandinavian rock carvings, pointing to the overwhelming predominance of outline carvings on Norwegian sites thought to be older. However, at Nämforsen he argues that the majority of scooped and outline carvings must be considered more or less contemporary. He regards very large outlined animals (see Figures 26 and 43) as probably the oldest. On this line of argument carving must have begun virtually simultaneously at a number of scattered points both along the river banks and on the islands.

Malmer (1975, 1981: 94–6) has produced the most detailed conventional chronology for Nämforsen, based on a pan-Scandinavian study of rock carvings. He extends Hallström's argument to claim that the majority, if not all, outline elks are older than the scooped forms. Pointing out that outline animals are more frequent on the islands, especially Brådön, than on the river banks, he goes on to suggest that rock carving may have been concentrated mainly on the islands in an earlier phase, and largely along the river shores later. Malmer relates the outline elks to the boat designs, claiming that it is the outline or double-line boat forms that are the earliest, with the single-line forms being carved later, again mainly along the river banks. Shoe soles are also considered by Malmer to be early, the circle–cross design on Brådön, and the humans with a triangular as opposed to a stick-line body (Malmer 1981: 97–8). He puts forward no specific chronological arguments concerning the fish or the birds. However, since these also appear in outline and scooped forms, the same type of argument might be applied. The Nämforsen material can then, according to Malmer, be broken down into two chronological groups:

Earlier	Later
outline elks	scooped elks
double-line boats	single-line boats
outline fish and birds?	scooped fish and birds?
humans with triangular body	humans with stick-line body
shoe soles	
circle–cross	

Malmer bases this argument for Nämforsen on two premises made explicit in relation to a consideration of Scandinavian boat designs taken as a whole: that 'those elements which occur most frequently are the earliest, and those which occur least frequently are the latest' (1981: 19) and that in 'prehistoric Northern Europe new impulses normally spread northwards from the south' (p. 21). Denmark is considered to be a 'natural innovation centre' for the Scandinavian Bronze Age (p. 22). Double-line boats can be dated here to an initial stage of the Bronze Age (Montelius period I) through cross-associations with designs on bronzes in graves. These designs then diffused north. Hallström also made attempts to trace southern Bronze Age 'influence' in the boat forms at Nämforsen. He claims that three double-lined boats have a clear southern Bronze Age character but regards the vast majority as having stylistic traits 'which seem to be original and autochthonic' (p. 295) and provides no arguments for regarding any single type of boat design at Nämforsen as necessarily older than any other type. Malmer states that all the boat forms at Nämforsen can easily be fitted into his boat typology classification system but this is not so surprising as Malmer's types are so generalized that almost any boat forms could be fitted into the appropriate slots. The only de*sign* forms that Malmer is prepared to grant an independent origin in northern Scandinavia are animal and bird forms (1981: 90), so we are left with two putative innovation centres, one for animals and birds in northern Scandinavia (diffusing south?) and another in the south encompassing boats, humans, shoe soles, etc.

As far as the elks are concerned, Malmer states that because the numerical frequencies of outline and scooped animals differ between the islands and the river banks this, of itself, 'demonstrates' that there is a time difference involved (1981: 96). Furthermore,

That type C [scooped animals] is in fact peculiar to Nämforsen indicates that it is the later form. C-type designs are poorly represented in the adjacent areas of the Scandinavian peninsula.

(Malmer 1981: 96)

All this naturally raises the question as to which motif types were carved at Nämforsen by the indigenous population without the benefit of ideas drawn, or received, from the outside. Malmer's answer (1981: 98) seems to be that at an early stage carving started at the site at a number of points, on the islands and on the river banks. Outline elks and triangular human bodies formed the basis of the repertoire of local motifs. Later, through external contact, double-lined boats, shoe soles and the circle–cross were introduced, with carving concentrating on the islands. The shoe soles and the circle–cross design never became popular at Nämforsen, while double-lined boats continued to be carved and became rapidly assimilated within local traditions, eventually giving rise to the single-line boat forms, with scooped elks replacing the outline elks. Malmer has nothing to say about the relationality or positioning of the carvings, apart from employing an island/river banks contrast. Presumably precisely where the carvings were executed and in relation to what other carvings are considered unimportant: a random process? This is borne out by the fact that throughout his book he discusses individual categories of motif types separately: ships, animals, hands, feet, etc., attempting to erect for each a chorological and chronological evolutionary trajectory.

Such arguments, based on diffusionist premises, coupled with a notion of a determinate and necessary evolution of carvings through a series of definite stages, suggests that the carvers at Nämforsen always produced outline animals first. Presumably, after many centuries of sleepless nights, or through further southern Bronze Age 'influence', they eventually stumbled upon the idea that animals might instead be carved out in scooped technique. We might ask: On what kind of psychological or social premises are Malmer's argument based? What are the 'influences' and why should the indigenous hunter-gatherer populations accept these 'influences' anyway? For Malmer 'influence' is a given. The materi-ality of the archaeological record is itself one of influence spread by movements of people or ideas. This just happens and the only relevant questions to be answered are those to do with the tem-porality and directionality of the 'influence'. The designs for Malmer might *mean* anything (p. 106) but whatever the meaning a motif always secretes an influence which through the passage of time generates others.

The specificity of the individual carved rock surfaces at Nämforsen, the relations between the designs, are simply compressed into tables of statistics. The only comparisons made are those between the islands and the river banks. But, as has already been pointed out, comparisons between the sentences on one page and those on the next are meaningless. Rather than making dubious statistical comparisons with rock carving surfaces hundreds, sometimes thousands, of kilometres away, we can regard the distinction between outline and scooped-out animals, single- and double-line boats, etc. at Nämforsen as a symbolic and aesthetic contrast, deliberately used to highlight definite associations, contrasts and relationships. Even if we were to accept certain links with southern Scandinavia which may have influenced motif form, these may have no necessary chronological relevance since, for example, an early southern Scandinavian boat design might have been deployed or used at Nämforsen at any stage in the production of the rock carvings there.

Malmer's arguments ignore entirely the very obvious relationships that exist between the carved de*signs* on individual carving surfaces – and here it might be appropriate to note again that actually reaching the central islands in the rapids must have been extremely dangerous and that many carvings were placed on precipitous surfaces, in places perhaps requiring scaffolding for their execution. Given these circumstances, a haphazard arrangement of motif forms, in which the execution of one bears no relation to another, seems highly unlikely even if, as has sometimes been suggested, the actual process of carving out the design was of great importance. In addition we may note with Hallström that although 'new figures may have been carved close to older ones ... A distinct consideration for the older carvings can nearly always be observed' (p. 308).

I do not want to give the impression that all Malmer's arguments can be dismissed outright but it does seem to be important to attempt to separate out two different parts of Malmer's arguments which become conflated in his account: (i) a valid and important emphasis on questions of culture contact and cultural change (see p. 51 and the discussion below pp. 158–64) and (ii) an unacceptable reliance on the rather dubious diffusionist principles that I have been concerned to criticize here.

Lindqvist (1978, 1983) has effectively reversed Malmer's arguments that the scooped-out de*signs* are older than those executed in outline technique. This argument is based on the altitude of the carvings and paintings in northern Scandinavia in relation to sea levels and land uplift. Lindqvist notes that scooped-out forms generally lie at a higher altitude (1978: 24ff.) than the outline forms. At Nämforsen, on the island of Brådön, the same pattern can be observed – outline forms are generally on carving surfaces at a higher level (84–79 m above sea level) compared to the outline forms (82–72 m above sea level (pp. 52–3). Both this position and Helskog's (1985, 1987) depend on the questionable assumptions that rock carvings were always executed immediately above the water line and when land uplift took place the newly exposed rock surfaces were then utilized and the older ones abandoned. Even if this were to be accepted, it is apparent from Lindqvist's own figures and diagrams that no absolute altitudinal differences between the location of outline and scooped forms are apparent at Nämforsen and indeed on Brådön, and on the other topographical carving pages outline and scooped forms regularly occur on the same carving surfaces, albeit often in differing relative frequencies. Lindqvist himself accepts that outline and scooped forms at Nämforsen do not represent clearly demarcated chronological phases and for much if not all of the carving period at the site both styles were in use (Lindqvist 1983: 9: diagram). Furthermore, if we compare the figures for outline and scooped forms in relation to altitude on Notön, the only 'chronological' pattern that emerges is that at an earlier stage scooped forms are more frequent and later this situation is reversed, with more outline forms occurring.

Part of the meaning of the outline and scooped elks, the single-line and double-line boats, etc., may be to do with transformations over time. I believe that Lindqvist is correct in regarding the scooped depictions as having an earlier origin or being more common at an earlier stage than the outline forms (see below p. 112) but we need to know why this happened. What seems to be of equal importance to the chronometric time in terms of which Malmer or Lindqvist frame their arguments is the timeless quality of the carvings. The same motifs are employed over and over again in an endless series of repetitions. That it is impossible to provide any detailed relative chronology for any individual elk, boat, shoe sole, etc. is not just our very contemporary 'failing': it may be telling us something of profound importance about the nature of the carved designs and their associations.

The time taken to execute a single carving by an artisan cannot have been very long, particularly in the case of the more stylized depictions, and even the largest carving surfaces might have been completed in a number of weeks, depending on the number of artisans involved. Naturally some carving surfaces must be earlier than others. On any individual carving surface it may still be the case that some motifs were carved first and others added later. Regardless of this, what we see today are the 'completed' and subsequently eroded carving surfaces. Irrespective of the time of execution of individual motif forms, at some stage they must have all acted together as symbolic units on individual rock surfaces and this is the palimpsest that we can perhaps best begin to understand. Two approaches may be taken here: (i) We can attempt an ahistorical analysis in which time is regarded as largely irrelevant to our overall understanding, i.e. we would deny that chronometric time is important, or alternatively that all we can hope to understand is the 'completed' site, i.e. the significance of Nämforsen when all carvings had been already executed. (ii) We could hope to incorporate some reference to chronometric temporality in the argument, given the limitations of the data, and build this into a wider analysis. Both of these approaches will be pursued in various parts of the text.

7

RELATED TEXTS

Any comparison of Nämforsen with other known carving sites in northern Sweden can only serve to underline both its enormity and its complexity, whether in terms of numbers of depictions, carving surfaces utilized, or the range and variety of designs employed. Fourteen other sites with rock carvings or paintings are known (Figure 21; Table 12). Of these, five are carving sites and seven have paintings. All the other sites are similarly dominated by the form of the elk and the identification of any other animal species remains uncertain, as at Nämforsen. Other designs are infrequent.

Human bodies occur at four other sites on six individual carving/painting surfaces. As at Nämforsen, they never occur in isolation but only in association with other designs, and always in relation to elks (with elks and boats at Stornorrfors; with elks and ambiguous boats/birds at Skärvången: Brattberget). None are phallic, hold or do anything, merge or conjoin with other designs. 'Triangular' or outline bodies occur at Flatruet and clearly recall those at Nämforsen. Those at the other sites are stick-line representations. Clearly identifiable boats occur only at Stornorrfors. These are depicted on carving surfaces with elks (in one case also with a human body). All are double-lined and five out of a total of seven possess internal hull division. Only one has an appended simplified animal (elk) head. None have any crew; one has appended 'crew strokes'. One of the boats is clearly superpositioned in relation to an elk that crosses it laterally.

Entirely missing from these other sites are shoe soles, fish, tools, single-line boats and a wide variety of double-lined boat forms found at Nämforsen. Designs on these other carving and painting sites which do not occur at Nämforsen include one possible snake depiction, a few abstract rhomboid or net patterns, elk and possibly human tracks at Gärdeforsen.

87

Table 12 Rock carving and painting sites in northern Sweden (Site numbers refer to Figure 21. Surf.= frequency of carving or painting surfaces.)

Site name	Map no.	Surf.	Motif categories							
			1	2	3	4	5	6	7	Total
Carving sites										
Gärdeforsen	1	4	5	–	4?	–	4?	–	–	13
Glösabäcken	2	5	43	–	–	–	–	–	2	45
Håltbergsudden	3	3	4	–	–	–	–	–	–	4
Landverk	4	1	4	–	–	–	–	–	–	4
Stornorrfors	5	6	27	2	7	–	–	–	–	36
Painting sites										
Åbosjön	6	1	1	–	–	–	–	–	–	1
Fångsjön	7	3	16	–	–	–	–	–	1	17
Flatruet	8	1	16	3	–	–	–	–	–	19
Grannberget	9	1	1	–	–	–	–	–	–	1
Hästskotjärn	10	5	6	–	–	–	–	1	–	7
Skärvången:										
Brattberget	11	1	2	2	–	3	–	–	–	7
Skärvången:										
Hällberget	12	6	8	7	–	–	–	–	2?	17
Storberget	13	3	4	–	–	–	–	–	1?	5
Brattforsen	14	1	2	–	–	–	–	–	–	2
Total:		41	139	14	11	3	4?	1	6	178

References: Sites 1–4: Hallström (1960); 5: Ramqvist, Forsberg and Backe (1985); 7–12: Hallström (1960); 13: Melander (1980); 14: Sundström (1982). Motif categories: 1: animals (elks); 2: humans; 3: boats; 4: birds; 5: animal tracks; 6: snakes; 7: ornamental (e.g. rhombs)

None of the elks at these sites are executed in scooped technique or as silhouettes. They are all executed in outline form. The absence of the depiction of antlers found at Nämforsen (and elks almost always with ears) is duplicated at these other sites. Only six of the elks at two sites, Brattforsen and Glösabäcken, possess clearly identifiable antlers but at these sites, both of which lack boats of any kind, there is no question of any ambiguous antler/single-line boat associations as at Nämforsen (Figure 34). The vast majority of the elks, as at Nämforsen, are also portrayed in profile with only two legs. However, large numbers of elks with three or four legs occur at Glösabäcken, as do a few depictions at Håltbergsudden and Stornorrfors. At these three sites it is very difficult to determine precisely how many legs are being depicted. However, it is interesting to note that front leg/back leg differentiation occurs, as at Nämforsen, and in some cases this is very marked. Some sites such as Stornorrfors are dominated by depictions of passive elks; at others active and passive animals occur in roughly equal numbers.

The major difference between many of the elks at these other carving and painting sites and the outline elks at Nämforsen is the presence of internal body divisions. All the bigger carving sites and most of the smaller ones (four exceptions) possess large numbers of elks with internal body division (Table 13). At Nämforsen elks with body division occur only on the central carving surface on Brådön (Figure 19), yet another feature which, in conjunction with the circle–cross motif, marks it out from all the others. In connection with the analysis of the elks at Nämforsen it has been suggested that at least some of the animals may have been depicted as a number of body parts. The presence of internal body divisions lends further support to this idea. The form of these body divisions has been systematically related to the internal organs and bone structure of the elk: ribs, heart, kidney, sexual organs by a number of archaeologists (Sörensen 1975; Bakka 1975; Ramqvist et al. 1985; Mikkelsen 1986). The elk is being portrayed in X-ray perspective (Figures 41 and 42). In relation to Nämforsen we need to ask why this occurs on only one carving surface, the one right at the centre of the site, and why it is so comparatively infrequent when other features of the depictions of elks at the other sites more or less mirror those found at Nämforsen, at least for outline forms.

Table 13 The frequencies of elks at rock carving and painting sites in northern Sweden possessing internal body division

Site name	No. of elks	No. with body divisions
Gärdeforsen	5	1
Glösabäcken	43	19
Landverk	4	4
Stornorrfors	27	24
Åbosjön	1	1
Fångsjön	16	8
Flatruet	16	5
Hästskotjärn	6	3
Skärvången:		
Hällberget	8	7
Brattforsen	2	1

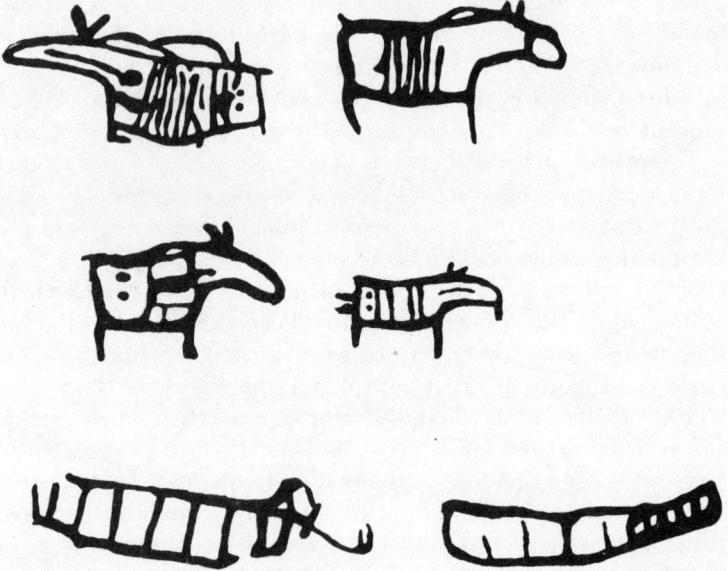

Figure 41 Examples of internal body division in elks and hull division in double-line boats from the rock carving site at Stornorrfors (Location: Figure 21, No. 5). Compare with diagram of skeletal structure and internal body organs of the elk (Figure 42). (Illustrations after Ramqvist, Forsberg and Backe 1985)

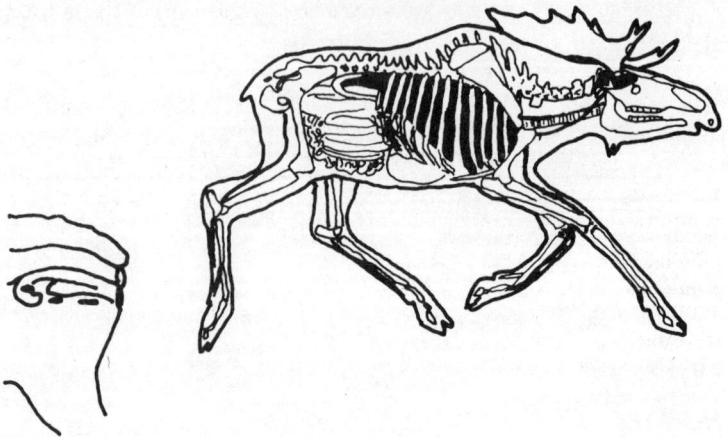

Figure 42 Cross-section of an elk showing skeletal structure, internal body organs and reproductive organs (inset) (Based on Mikkelsen 1987: Figure 8 and Ramqvist, Forsberg and Backe: Figure 25)

Figure 43 Rock carving surface, Notön (Location: Figure 16, No. 5. Source: Hallström 1960: Plate XXI: R: 3. Scale: 1: 20).

Another huge elk dominates this carving surface consisting of six to seven elks and six to seven boats. However, unlike the surface on Brådön, on which there is an exceptionally large elk (Figure 26), this is not a simple display of motifs and their relational importance. All the boats with elk head prows face right while the elks face left. The larger three central elks appear in more or less active poses with their legs bent. One of these opposes a double-line boat with simplified animal (elk) head prow. In the body of another an elk head is displayed. The largest elk is intersected by three boats, the largest and most complete of which is superpositioned on its head. Remains of a smaller boat cut across the outline in the region of the heart, while a third (portrayed upside-down) overlaps in the region of the uterus. The boat–elk overlap in these three vital areas, together with the possible depiction of a pregnant elk to the right and the clear opposition between elk and boat to the left, provides further confirmation of an intimate connection between elks and boats and, in this case, an additional right–left association.

Beyond these differences and similarities between the depictions at Nämforsen and elsewhere there exists a striking series of regularities in the location of the carving sites. All are situated on or near to precipitous cliffs and only two (Grannberget and Storberget, both with very limited numbers of depictions) are not located immediately next to water, on lake shores (eight sites) or along streams or rivers (four sites). The sites by the lakes are located on the bases of cliffs licked by the waters and immediately above the waterline. The carvings at Glösabäcken are situated 500 m from a lake along the course of a stream by a waterfall. At low water some of the carvings are splashed, while at highest water all the carvings are submerged (Hallström 1960: 64). The carvings at Gärdeforsen and Stornorrfors are both situated in islands in river channels at the sites of a series of rapids in a manner directly analogous to Nämforsen.

The Stornorrfors site is of particular interest in this respect. It has already been noted that it is the only site apart from Nämforsen possessing boat de*signs*. Like Nämforsen at the time during which the carvings were executed, the rapids surrounding them would have been the last before the river entered an inlet of the open sea (Ramqvist *et al.* 1985: 316). On the river bank in the immediate vicinity of the site is an unusually large settlement site (unexcavated) estimated to cover an area of at least 150 × 100 m and almost certainly occupied on a recurrent basis over a long time period (Ramqvist *et al.* 1985: 318). Water and violent rapids are intimately bound up with the meaning and significance of the de*signs*.

Part II

MEDIATING THE TEXT

8

A STRUCTURAL LOGIC

Significative systems, whether in language or non-verbal material form, are rarely simple. They spread out in terms of paradigmatic series and syntagmatic chains, and a static one-to-one correlation between signifier and signified in an overall structural system, as originally envisaged by Saussure, can be regarded as perhaps more the exception than the rule, especially with regard to a material significative medium, or literary uses of language. Sign systems have an inherent tendency to polysemy (sets of different meanings) and a condensation of meaning within an individual signifier. The same material sign may change its meaning across time and space. Its meaning will alter according to who is using it and why, the context in which it appears, the audience to which it is directed and who interprets it. This being stated, it needs to be underlined that Saussure's stress on the arbitrary relation between signifier and signified in language needs to be considerably modified in relation to material culture. It is necessary to distinguish between different poles and types of material signification. In order to understand the nature of significative processes in material culture we need to bear in mind that:

1 signification is grounded in tradition;
2 signification is rooted in social relations and social structures;
3 signs will differ according to their degree of polysemy and the social context in which they are used;
4 signification in material culture is generally much simpler than in either spoken or written language.

Our relation to language is one of necessity. If we wish to be understood it is necessary to abide by rules of syntax and grammar. However, within language any competent user can generate new sentences and still be confident that he or she will be comprehensible. This is patently not the case with material culture, in which there is a much greater degree of restriction resulting from customary practices which determine what can be 'said'. The generation of fresh material culture 'sentences' is a much less fluid process. Material culture gains significance through its social usage, and the form of signification, to be effective, requires repetitive use. A sign used only once would be no sign at all. Signs do not occur in isolation but always in paradigmatic series and syntagmatic chains, for their meaning depends on differences from others, and these 'series' and 'chains' cross-cut and inform each other.

BRICOLAGE, CLASSIFICATORY SYSTEMS

In his major work on systems of classification in small-scale non-western societies Lévi-Strauss (1966) introduced the image of the *bricoleur*, the closest English equivalent of which is an inveterate do-it-yourself person who performs various patching up and construction tasks with whatever materials happen to be at hand: a screw may be used when a nail is lacking, a hacksaw substituted for a wood saw. The *bricoleur* is a person who, in short, makes do with whatever material is at hand to achieve a given end. The set of heterogeneous instruments and materials used by the *bricoleur* to perform the task in hand is closed and he or she has to make do with what is available, which may bear no direct relation to the current or any future project. The contingent results of the tasks engaged in by the *bricoleur* supply him or her with fresh or renewed instruments and materials from the various construction and demolition projects engaged in. Things are kept because they may be of use at a later date rather than with a particular set of future tasks in view. The *bricoleur* does not possess specialized tools in relation to, say, various specific and delimited plumbing or carpentry projects; his or her means and materials are more generalized, having operational or multifunctional use in relation to different situations (Lévi-Strauss 1966: 17–18). *Bricolage* is the act of using and adapting existing elements in a fresh way. It is a vital component of what Lévi-Strauss calls the 'untamed mind', permitting means to be transformed into ends and vice versa. Associations and meanings are created through repeated acts of *bricolage* that build on each other. In this activity the untamed mind remains fundamentally different from contemporary forms of 'scientific' western consciousness and rationality in industrialized societies, which are dependent on a high degree of specialization in both materials and means (calculus, abstract symbolic logic) to perform specific tasks. One primary difference between *bricolage* and western thought is conceived by Lévi-Strauss in terms of goal orientation (1966: 19), itself restricted by differing forms of logic. An engineer is constrained in precisely the same manner as a *bricoleur* in that the execution of any task is dependent on prior sets of theoretical and practical knowledge, restricting possible solutions. However, the engineer will try to transcend existing constraints while the *bricoleur* is happy to work within the confines of an existing operational set. This difference arises because the engineer employs an abstract theoretical symbol set with which to approach the world whereas the *bricoleur* employs preconstituted sign systems. The fundamental opposition Lévi-Strauss proposes is that between concepts and signs. The engineer employs the former, the *bricoleur* the latter. Conceptual systems open up the set of possibilities and perspectives. Sign systems, on the other hand, work by a process of reorganization which, while being transformational in nature, does not renew or extend the set being worked on. Such systems demand that human culture be actively imposed on reality, rather than separated from it according to abstract principles. The *bricoleur* communicates both with signs and through their medium. The engineer orders the world, generalizes and solves problems, through a science of the abstract. The *bricoleur*'s knowledge is a science of the concrete. These remain two different ways in which to approach the world, give sense to it, and solve problems. The relationship between these two approaches is not evolutionary or progressive. Each is equally valid according to differing social and historical circumstances. Furthermore, one system does not replace the other; *bricolage* is of essential importance in the constitution of day-to-day practices in all societies. For Lévi-Strauss it is a distinctively *human* quality to think in this manner, when one is not following a restrictive series of 'scientific' rules.

In *The Savage Mind* Lévi-Strauss remarks that there is 'a sort of fundamental antipathy between history and systems of classification. This perhaps explains what one is tempted to call the "totemic void", for in the bounds of the great civilizations of Europe and Asia there is a remarkable absence of anything which might have reference to totemism, even in the form of remains' (1966: 232). I shall argue here that Nämforsen and northern Scandinavian rock carving sites effectively fill this totemic void, totemism being conceived, after Lévi-Strauss, as a term to be given to a particular form of social classificatory logic.

The site of Nämforsen can be regarded as a prime example of the untamed or non-domesticated human mind at work, a classic case of *bricolage*. A system designed to create meaning and significance and itself constituting social reality has been fashioned out of a disparate series of fragments and materials, some arising in the life experiences of the northern hunter-gatherers using the site, others derived from the contingency of external historical events and circumstances. Nämforsen demonstrates the manner in which a coherent and logical classificatory system can withstand and incorporate the vicissitudes of time and circumstance. The de*signs* at Nämforsen create and establish specific social categories and sets of relations or linkages between these categories. Their meaning is totemic in so far as we regard totemism as merely being an aspect of wider systems of categorization. The de*signs* involve both an anthropomorphization, or humanization, of nature and a physiomorphization, or natural-ization, of humanity. They involve a series of perspectives in which humanity and the natural world reflect each other and help to establish each other, as if reflections in a set of mirrors. The carvings actively utilize features drawn from the natural world, such as animal species, and objects drawn from the cultural world to create and maintain differentiation in the social world. The de*signs* at Nämforsen are not being chosen to depict animals because they are good to eat but because they are good to think with. They are being manipulated as parts of sign systems with connotative meanings going beyond themselves. The animal species and the cultural objects depicted are being utilized as signs of social differentiation. Perceptible and, as it were, ready-made differences in the natural world (those existing between animal species) and those existing between cultural objects and between cultural objects and natural species are being utilized to map out and help to sustain and differentiate between different social groups using Nämforsen.

ENCODING INFORMATION

I shall discuss two sets of logical possibilities which attempt to show de*sign* relationships as signifying sets of social relations between groups of hunter-fisher-gatherers using Nämforsen to encode information. It is this structural principle for helping us to understand the form and significance of the de*signs* that is of importance – the details of the particular schemes suggested are of course open to modification in a large number of different directions. What follow, then, are two interpretative experiments.

Excluding the human depictions, the six other de*sign* categories utilized clearly fall into two groups, one constituted on the basis of species differentiation, the other in terms of differences between manufactured cultural objects. Both of these sets are then linked back together on a metaphorical plane in terms of a series of signified natural elements in which each initial natural or cultural set duplicates the other on another plane:

Nature			Culture		
elk (land)	fish (salmon) (water)	bird (sky)	shoe sole ? (land) .	boat (water)	tool ? (sky) .

Each of the de*signs* at Nämforsen signifies a different hunter-gatherer clan utilizing the site. The differences between the two series of de*signs*, based respectively on species and object differentiation, suggest perhaps two moieties each subdivided into three clans, each of which is named by an animal or cultural object symbolizing a natural element. The overall relationship being symbolically represented on the carving surfaces is therefore

elk : fish : bird :: shoe sole : boat : tool

or elk is to fish is to bird as shoe sole is to boat is to tool. The de*signs* on the carving surfaces encode and display relationships between different moieties and clans utilizing the site. There do not seem to be any logical problems in connecting elks with land or fish with water. Birds, however, are clearly anomalous since they can live on land, water or in the sky. This anomaly is exactly duplicated in the cultural series. While shoe soles are only useful on land and boats on water, tools may be utilized on the land, in the water or in the air.

We are now beginning to understand the classificatory logic structuring the carving site at Nämforsen and it becomes apparent why the human de*signs* never occur on their own as isolated depictions on individual carving surfaces. This is because they do not fit into the logic of the system, which is based on mapping natural and cultural categories onto social groups. It would clearly defeat the internal logic of such a system to utilize the de*sign* of the human. So while the other de*signs* signify relations between different social groups or clans forming distinct moieties we need to ask what the human depictions signify.

The rock carving surfaces at Nämforsen are very definitely 'cold' in that we do not have much evidence for dynamism or change – the same limited number of de*signs* is employed over and over again. Why representational de*signs* were chosen rather than abstract depictions also becomes clear in that we are dealing with a cultural logic employing the concrete and the particular (individual species or cultural objects) as a means to map out social relations. The differences between elk and salmon are being exploited to signify social difference among hunter-gatherers in terms of both activities and lifestyle. Social difference is being created and maintained through mapping onto human groups perceptible differences in the real world.

In terms of the activity of carving we can regard the execution of any particular de*sign* (e.g. an individual elk) as an act of *parole* whose meaning and significance is governed by an underlying *langue* of rock carving in general. This *langue* or generative grammar is governed by the need to signify in material form the sets of relations between social groups utilizing the carving site and it is only on the central carving surface on Brådön that the entire set of connotative signs is brought together and displayed in its entirety. What is of interest here, as already has been pointed out (see p. 21 above), is not quantities of different de*sign* classes but their differences and their relationships on the carving surfaces.

Nämforsen is then all about the creation of a series of homologies between two parallel series of animal species and manufactured objects and social groups. A formal correlation is being constructed between two systems of differences, each constituting a pole of opposition. But we know the site is a palimpsest with de*signs* accumulating over time. Why were just *these* de*signs* adopted to construct sets of differences?

TIME AND STRUCTURE

Lévi-Strauss (1966: Chapter 8) comments that in 'totemic' classificatory systems there is always a tendency for the grammar to degenerate through time into a lexicon. This is because, unlike other classificatory systems which are primarily conceived (e.g. myths) or acted (e.g. rituals), a totemic classificatory system is *lived* on a continuous basis linking concrete social groups to concrete items (animals, objects) in the world. There is a conflict between the structural nature of the classificatory system and its statistical demographic basis, which may disrupt it through, for example, the expansion or decimation or alteration of various related social groups. In this antagonistic relation between structure and event, totemic classifications may change in order to incorporate temporality and, to a certain extent, to annul it.

At Nämforsen it is the natural *designs* that are indigenous: elks, fish and birds. Elks dominate all the other carving sites in northern Sweden while the other two occur with any certainty only at Nämforsen itself. What is the logic that links these species and not others, for example the bear or the wolf or the beaver or the eagle, in a relational system apart from their putative connection with differing natural elements? Such a problem could only be solved by recourse to native mythologies which are, of course, no longer available to us. However, such mythologies are often simply a matter of rationalizing the contingency of choices that have already been made. One common feature that does link the elk, fish (salmon) and bird together is that they all inhabit wet places: the elk is a quadruped favouring swampy locations, the birds depicted at Nämforsen appear to be swimmers: ducks, herons or swans. The fact that elks are the only animals which can be identified suggests that not only are virtually all the depictions of elk but that elks are being used to *represent* animals. In other words the elk (the largest species of animal) becomes the paradigm for and of the animal kingdom. This should not surprise us. Among the Osage, a southern Sioux group, the body of the elk 'is a veritable *imago mundi*: its coat represents grass, its hams hills, its flanks plains, its backbone the skyline, its neck valleys and its antlers the whole hydrographic network' (Lévi-Strauss 1966: 59). The last point about the antlers is of particular pertinence, given the ambiguous antler–boat association that has already been pointed out. In connection with this discussion of the elk, it is interesting to note that distinct species of fish (apart from the salmon) or other species living in water such as seals or porpoises are also impossible to recognize. The salmon is a fish that leaps in the air and is thus 'higher' than any other fish just as the elk is higher than any other land animal inhabiting northern Sweden. It thus becomes the paradigm form for water living creatures. Birds which may live on land, water and in the air form a more anomalous category than animals which can live only on land or fish confined to water. But, as mentioned previously, the birds depicted do appear to be swimmers. They are both in the water and above it and may frequent dry land. They link together the elk and the salmon through their anomalous behaviour and through their flight they are also 'high'.

The very heterogeneity in the classificatory structure utilized at Nämforsen, i.e. the fact that it is divided into a natural and a cultural series and that the terms constituting the natural series can all be locally derived, whereas some of those making up the cultural series, such as shoe soles and some of the boat forms, are only very common outside the Nämforsen area in southern Scandinavia, suggests that the system may be derivative here and adapted to fit in with a pre-existing classificatory structure. So we might add to the pre-existing scheme by relating it to another set of oppositions nature : culture :: inside : outside :: elk : fish : bird :: shoe sole : boat : tool.

In postulating such a structural order we run the risk of ignoring the detail of the de*sign* forms, in particular the different types of elks and boats and tools. To reach a satisfactory solution to the problem of how these are related requires the incorporation of this detail within a structural model. While we know the human de*signs* have relational significance only to other types of de*signs*, this also requires further investigation.

The most frequent de*signs* are the elk and the boat and we might profitably begin the investigation by looking more closely at the relations between these two de*sign* classes.

PRINCIPLES LINKING ELKS AND BOATS

I have argued that in the almost universal absence of antlers the elks depicted signify a female principle (p. 68). This observation may be taken further by suggesting that

elk: boat :: female: male

or elk is to boat as female is to male. The elk and the boat are connotative signs and represent female and male respectively. This is part of their meaning and human society is being portrayed as in part dependent for its reproduction on this opposition. Although there are good grounds for the argument that elks do in fact signify a female principle, we need to investigate what basis there is for suggesting that boats represent a corresponding male principle. First, there are transformational relations of similarity in boat and elk depictions. Second, there are definite regularities in spatial patterning and arrangements and cases of boat–elk conjunctions. These can be considered in more detail.

A: similarities in depictions of elk and boat

- Virtually all boats possess a naturalistic or simplified elk head. That these are elk heads is particularly marked on the single-line boat (see Figure 39). A definite connection is being forged between elks (female) and boats.
- I have noted that in a very few cases elks are depicted with antlers but these antler depictions are virtually identical to those of single-line boats (Figure 34).
- Just as there are some cases of two-headed elks, some single-line boats possess an elk head at either end.

B: regularities in spatial patterning

- Groupings of boats are depicted in exactly the same way as elks. There are herds of elks and 'herds' of boats (e.g. Figures 40, 44).
- For the entire Nämforsen area both elks and boats are more frequently depicted facing right or west than left or east. Few elks or boats are aligned on a north–south axis. This right–left distinction is, however, only particularly marked *and* consistent for both elks and boats on page IV, the eastern island of Notön (Table 14).

Table 14 Frequencies of elks and boats facing right and left according to topographical carving pages

	Page I	Page II	Page III	Page IV	Total
Right elks	113	11	80	114	318
Left elks	90	10	98	82	280
Right boats	11	21	12	94	138
Left boats	10	7	11	48	76

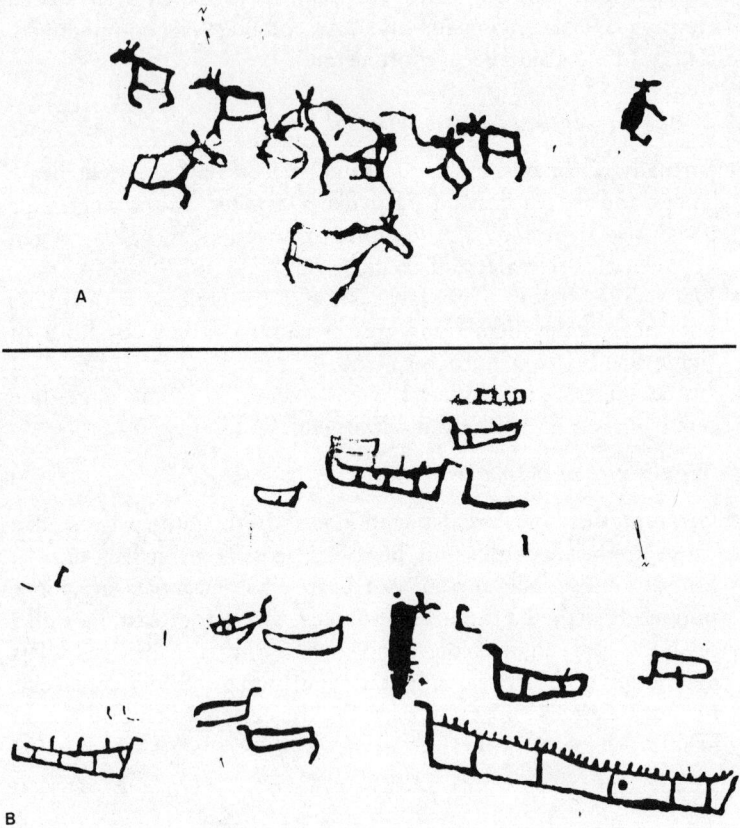

Figure 44 Herds of elks and 'herds' of boats on two rock carving surfaces at Nämforsen (Scale: 1:20). A: Brådön (Source: Hallström 1960: Plate XXIV: D: 1); B: Notön (Source: Hallström 1960: Plate XVIII: E: 2)

- On individual carving surfaces on which only elks and boats are depicted a systematic relation of dispersion occurs involving:

  (i) Linearity: Elks and boats may be aligned in rows either horizontally or vertically.

  (ii) Superpositioning: Elks and boats may be superimposed.

  (iii) Opposition: Elks and boats may be systematically structured in relation to each other.

- Conjunctions: Throughout the Nämforsen material there are cases in which elks and boats are combined into a complex multiple figure in addition to cases of superimposition.
- The elks and boats appear to be spatially related to the human depictions. On carving surfaces (e.g. Figure 33) where what is being stressed is an elk–human relation the boats are in a marginal position.
- These principles of linearity, superpositioning, merging and opposition may be combined with each other in various ways (see Figure 45 and cf. Figures 19, 23, 24, 25, 38). All these forms of elk–boat combinations are also found on rock carving surfaces where motifs other than elks and boats also occur.

In short, from the nine points discussed above there appears to be overwhelming evidence to suggest a consistent series of definite elk–boat relationships which, in the absence of male elk depictions and in view of a highly ambiguous elk antler–single-line boat association, can be made more coherent as a relationship between male and female.

Where do human figures and the other designs, then, fit into this picture and the set of oppositions which may now be built up?

Clan A : Clan B
elk : boat
land : water
nature : culture
inside : outside

A series of elk–boat relations has been established in a general way but how does this relate to the two major categories of elk and boat forms: the outline and scooped elks and the single- and double-line boats? Considered in terms of a combinatorial grammar, there are nine different possibilities which can initially be considered in terms of those rock carving surfaces on which only elks and boats occur (Table 15) but not all of these combinations are being exploited. The system is being restricted to only certain combinational possibilities. If the two forms of elk occur together they may be associated with single- or double-line boats but if both boat forms occur on the same carving surface then the two elk forms must also occur together. Outline elks only occur in isolation with double-line boats. In general, then, we may state the relationship between the two forms of elk and boat as being:

outline elk: scooped elk :: double-line boat: single-line boat

This relationship is also indicated by other features:

1 The clearest cases of conjunction or merging between elks and boats involve scooped elks and single-line forms *or* double-line boats and outline elks (see Figure 45).
2 The most naturalistic elk forms are scooped while it is the single-line boats that possess clearly identifiable as opposed to heavily stylized elk-head prows (see e.g. Figure 46).
3 In cases involving superpositioning or relational oppositions on individual carving surfaces on which only elks and boats occur this involves in almost all cases scooped elks and double-line boats *or* outline elks and single-line boats (see e.g. Figures 45, 23, 24).

Table 15 The frequencies of grammatically possible different de*sign* combinations on carving surfaces on which only elks and boats occur

Design combination	Frequency
scooped elk + single-line boat	3
outline elk + single-line boat	0
scooped elk + double-line boat	6
outline elk + double-line boat	19
scooped elk + outline elk + single-line boat	3
scooped elk + outline elk + double-line boat	3
scooped elk + single-line boat + double-line boat	0
outline elk + single-line boat + double-line boat	0
scooped elk + outline elk + single-line boat + double-line boat	2

Having established a set of relations between different elk and boat forms, we may attempt to relate this to the other de*sign* forms at Nämforsen. Again we may initially consider these relationships in terms of carving surfaces on which elks or boats occur in association with only one other motif category or in terms of other direct associations. Five significant sets of relations can be noted:

1 Shoe soles occur only with outline elks.
2 Shoe soles occur only with double-line boats.
3 Fish occur only with double-line boats. In these cases the fish are in outline as opposed to scooped forms. The scooped forms occur

Figure 45 Types of elk–boat associations from different carving surfaces at Nämforsen on which only elks and boats occur. A: linearity; B and C: opposition; D: linearity and opposition; F: linearity, opposition and superpositioning; E: three examples of merging elks and boats taken from different carving surfaces

Figure 46 Rock carving surface, northern river banks (Location: Figure 13, No. 4. Source: Hallström 1960: Plate XIII: G: 1)

on carving surfaces with large numbers of scooped elks and other designs.

4 Elk heads on poles occur only in single-line boats.

5 Stick-line humans are primarily associated with single-line boats, triangular humans with double-line boats.

On the basis of these associations we may formulate the following binary sets:

outline elk	:	scooped elk
double-line boat	:	single-line boat
outline fish	:	scooped fish
shoe soles	:	elk heads on poles
triangular humans	:	stick humans

Birds which appear only on carving surfaces with a large number of motif categories and tools such as scythes have no clear relational associations and cannot be inserted into this system in terms of de*sign* relationships alone.

A number of features distinguish the stick-line and triangular human figures in terms of distinctive associations that need to be drawn into the account:

1 The two forms occur together only twice on individual carving surfaces: once on Brådön and once on Notön.

2 Two of the 'triangular' figures hold scythe-like tools, otherwise they do not hold or do anything. The stick-line figures, by contrast, hold 'scythes', poles, elk heads on poles, spears and other implements in some cases. They are clearly more diverse in terms of activities depicted.

3 The stick-line figures occur on boats (single- and double-line) on a small number of carving surfaces but the vast majority of their associations are with elks, not with boats. They merge with elks, carry elks, herd elks, hold elk heads on poles.

4 The only clear phallic representations are on the stick-line figures. In all cases these figures are in intimate association with elks and in a couple of examples carry elk-head poles. It is only the stick-line figures which are involved in love scenes.

Some generalized spatial contrasts in the distribution of de*signs* at Nämforsen need to be drawn into the account. One of the major contrasts is between page IV (the island of Notön, downriver, furthest to the east and closest to the sea) and pages I–III, both in

SINGLE MOIETY ORGANIZATION (STICK-LINE HUMANS)

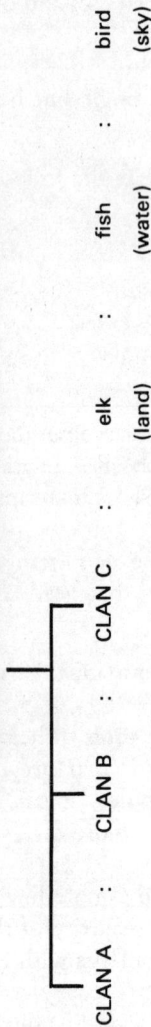

PHASE A

```
        ┌──────────────┴──────────────┐
   ┌────┴────┐                         │
CLAN A  :  CLAN B  :  CLAN C  :   elk    :   fish    :   bird
                                 (land)     (water)     (sky)
```

DUAL MOIETY ORGANIZATION

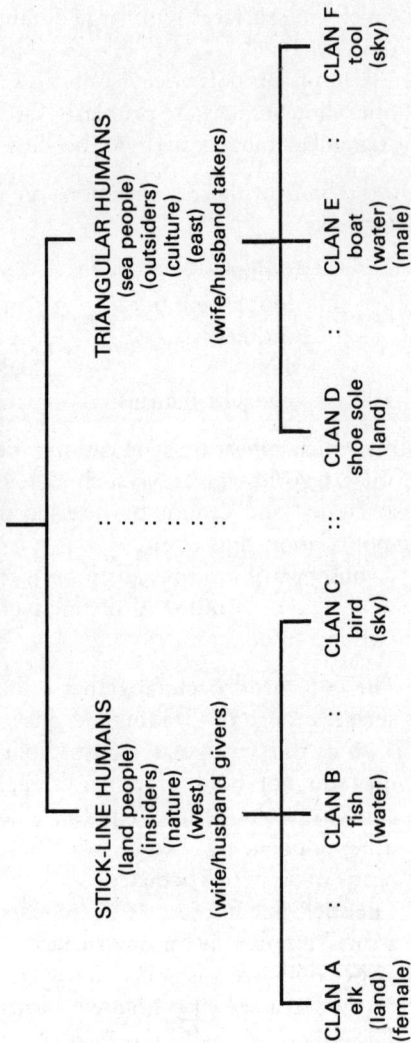

PHASE B

```
                    ┌─────────────────────────────┴─────────────────────────────┐
        STICK-LINE HUMANS                                          TRIANGULAR HUMANS
        (land people)                                              (sea people)
        (insiders)                                                 (outsiders)
        (nature)                                                   (culture)
        (west)                                                     (east)
        (wife/husband givers)          ::                          (wife/husband takers)
                                       ::
                                       ::
                                       ::
   ┌────────┴────────┐                                      ┌──────────┴──────────┐
CLAN A  :  CLAN B  :  CLAN C                           CLAN D   :   CLAN E   :   CLAN F
 elk       fish       bird                           shoe sole    boat          tool
(land)    (water)    (sky)                            (land)     (water)       (sky)
(female)                                                         (male)
```

PHASE C *either* (1)

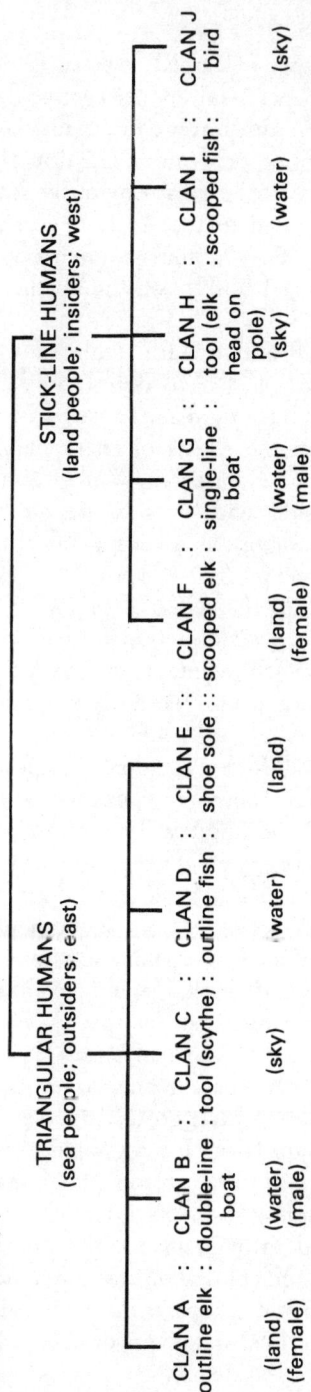

TRIANGULAR HUMANS
(sea people; outsiders; east)

| CLAN A | : | CLAN B | : | CLAN C | : | CLAN D | : | CLAN E | :: | CLAN F | : | CLAN G | : | CLAN H | : | CLAN I | : | CLAN J |
| outline elk | | double-line boat | | tool (scythe) | | outline fish | | shoe sole | | scooped elk | | single-line boat | | tool (elk head on pole) | | scooped fish | | bird |

STICK-LINE HUMANS
(land people; insiders; west)

(land)
(female)

(water)
(male)

(sky)

(water)

(land)

(land)
(female)

(water)
(male)

(sky)

(water)

(sky)

or (2)

STICK-LINE HUMANS
(land people; insiders; west)

CLAN A	:	CLAN B
outline elk		double-line boat
(land)		(water)
(female)		(male)

::

TRIANGULAR HUMANS
(sea people; outsiders; east)

CLAN C	:	CLAN D
scooped elk		single-line boat
(land)		(water)
(female)		(male)

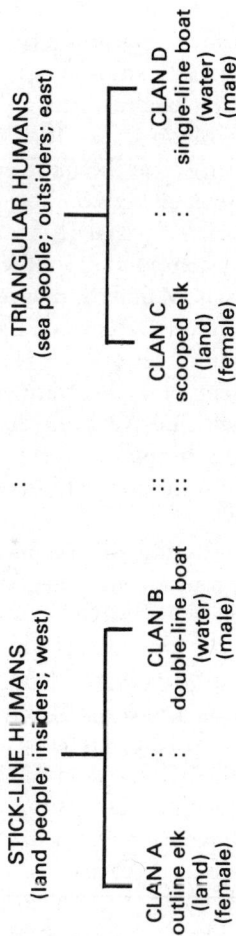

Figure 47 Model of chronological sequence of structural oppositions used at Nämforsen

terms of motif representation and types of carved rock surfaces. While 68 per cent of the elks are on pages I–III, 65 per cent of the boats are on page IV. Human bodies with outline or 'triangular' body form occur with only one exception on Notön. The double-line boats comprise what can be taken to be most obviously sea-going vessels (e.g. Figure 39), as opposed to the single-line ones which appear more as river canoes. They dominate on carving surfaces situated furthest to the west and upriver on the northern river banks.

Malmer put forward a possible chronology for some of the designs at Nämforsen and suggested, as I have done above, a division between those with an indigenous origin and those perhaps being derived from outside as part of the effects of an exchange system linking southern Scandinavia and Nämforsen. While I think that Malmer's division between 'inside' and 'outside' designs is essentially correct, I concur with Lindqvist in reversing his temporal series (see the discussion on pp. 80–6 above). These temporal observations can be built into the series of oppositions which have been discussed above to provide a transformational diachronic set of structural oppositions whose intent is to mark out and differentiate between social groups using Nämforsen (Figure 47).

Putting all this into a narrative: Nämforsen is initially used by groups of hunter-gatherers with a single moiety organization composed of three clans (the terms 'clan' and 'moiety' I am aware are well-worn terms which may be held to carry an unnecessarily heavy anthropological load. I use them here as short-hand terms describing, respectively, the localized groupings of persons in domestic units and to refer to a wider supralocal level of organization linking these units together). Each clan differentiates itself, mapping interclan relations by exploiting differences between natural species, each connected with a natural element. So clan A is to clan B is to clan C as elk is to fish is to bird (phase A). In phase B the carving site begins to be utilized by different hunter-gatherer groups involved in exchange relations with southern Scandinavian farming populations, differentiating themselves by utilizing cultural objects rather than natural species to emphasize both moiety and clan differentiation. Moiety differentiation is emphasized through use of the human body as a design while animal species and cultural objects differentiate between the clans, subdivided into two groups (male and female) according to whether they are wife or husband givers or takers. In phase C this whole clan organization expands and simultaneously the utilization of natural or cultural objects as connotative signs symbolizing clan differentiation breaks down. Differences are then expressed through the same limited range of traditional motifs, sometimes based on the style of their execution (as scooped or outline forms). Each clan becomes simultaneously differentiated in terms of 'male' or 'female', i.e. whether they give or take wives or husbands in marriage exchanges. An alternative scenario is that the system contracts, with the result that the de*sign* forms are no longer utilized, apart from elks and boats, again differentiated by the technique of execution of the design on the carving surfaces as a means of signifying different clan relations. This might go some way to resolve a logical difficulty in the account that has been given. Elks and boats dominate quantitatively and in relation to other de*sign* forms (superpositioning, similitude, etc.), and it may be inadequate therefore to assign them the same significative status as the other de*signs*. If I am right that elk: boat :: female: male then this is a fundamental opposition and there do not appear to be any exactly equivalent oppositions between other de*sign* classes.

9

AN HERMENEUTICS
OF MEANING

The previous chapter left out a number of features vital to the understanding of Nämforsen. It became increasingly unconvincing the more it tried to compress the details of the designs into a single and all-embracing scheme. Content has in fact been considered only in so far as it has been compressed into form and in parts of the exposition there has been a quite clear and probably unacceptable tendency towards a one-to-one mapping of meaning and structure onto social organization. In addition, the specificity of de*sign* patterning, at least on the more complex carving surfaces, has not been adequately considered. At this point in the analysis I will attempt a movement away from the analysis of de*sign* relationships at a structural level to develop an hermeneutics of meaning content, discussing aspects of the work of Gadamer and Ricoeur, the two principal exponents of hermeneutic theory working today.

The structural analysis, it might be claimed, merely constitutes a depth descriptive interpretation of some aspects of carving form, along with an imputed classificatory or totemic significance in which the carvings signify sets of social relations. This, in fact, might be taken to represent a starting point rather than a finishing point for analysis, the textual inscription of an initial arc in a more comprehensive hermeneutic spiral through which the subjectivity of the archaeologist and the objectivity of the rock carvings become fused in the production of a discourse which of necessity opens out the way to the production of others in a continuous process of grafting meaning.

114

INTERPRETATION AND MEANING

For Gadamer (1975) understanding always and of necessity takes place from the point of view of the person who wants to interpret. A historical understanding of texts cannot consist in an attempt to relive the processes of their production and the contexts in which they were produced. Any approach based on an empathetic mode of thought in which the self is simply to be transposed in terms of the historic or anthropological 'other' can only result in illusion, self-deception. Furthermore, the very conception of oneself as a 'person' with a distinctive consciousness and approach to the world is itself an hermeneutic act. Trying to understand oneself is a process parallel to understanding others. Interpretation is, in effect, always a process of reinterpretation, something which takes place from the vantage point of the present, of the here and now. This, for Gadamer, is an ontological maxim that cannot be questioned. It is part of the nature of human existence and by no means implies that we move inexorably between a position in which we realize that the text has no ultimate, fully gounded or certain meaning to one in which any meaning is claimed to be as good as any other, a hyperrelativism in which there is no way of choosing between one interpretation and another.

Gadamer proposes an 'effective history'. This involves (1) an awareness of one's own hermeneutic situation and the sociohistorical 'horizon' in which it is embedded; (2) a dialogic relationship between the interpreter and the text; (3) a dialectic of question and answer in the process of understanding texts; (4) an openness to tradition: all knowledge emerges from the investigator's place within a tradition of understanding which is derived from the past and from which prejudices arise.

The fundamental question becomes not whether we can avoid a certain degree of relativism, which is clearly impossible as we cannot neatly circumvent ourselves or our social situation as interpreters, but how relativist we should be. It simply is not rational to reject relativism. The notion of an absolute free-floating Reason transcending all persons and social conditions is in fact itself only the product of a particular historical set of circumstances grounded in Enlightenment belief. Understanding, for Gadamer, goes far beyond the actions of a subject, since what the subject regards as worth knowing (his or her prejudice) is itself determined by research traditions. Gadamer, in effect, argues for a conditionalist thesis in which the text breaks and actively resists our interpretations. It is impossible to say anything at all about it and we in fact do have criteria for choosing between alternative statements. A materialist notion is retained of the text in itself containing its own meanings, as against those simply grafted on by the reader. A historical consciousness involves collision and incompatibility between the text and the reader, an experience of tension between the past and the present. The hermeneutic task consists of bringing this tension out rather than attempting to paper over the cracks, to sublimate it. Out of the tension will arise a 'fusion of horizons' between subject and object, past and present. In this fusion the presuppositions of the reader and the text's internal claims to truth become conjoined. This fusion is permitted, according to Gadamer, by linguistic experience. Our experience of the world is always pre-formed by language so that language becomes indelibly part of our being in the world, a point where 'I' and the world meet (1975: 431): 'Being that can be understood is language' (1975: 432). All understanding is therefore linguistic. Language is not a tool or resource we use but a medium through which we must work. Gadamer leaves us with a perpetual present–past and subject–object dialectic fused through linguistic capabilities in which neither has any priority or more secure claim to truth. Subject and object, past and present (like *langue* and *parole*) are two sides of the same coin.

A very significant point is that, rather than attempting to banish the historically situated interpreter, Gadamer wants to elevate his or her role in the process of creating meaning. To interpret means to 'use one's own preconceptions so that the meaning of the text can really be made to speak for us' (1975: 358). Furthermore, no text can speak for us unless it speaks in a language that can reach the other person. In other words interpretation is endless, bound up with tradition, and changes in relation to the situation in which understanding is taking place. Understanding is a process in which we need to try out alternative readings of the text to see how to make sense of it from different positions. It involves questions and answers, making choices, being prepared to change one's position to open out fresh possibilities. To understand is to translate, to bring out certain aspects which seem important in the text while inevitably placing others to one side, emphasizing what appears to be impor-tant. Understanding is an ongoing process. As such it can never achieve ontological finality. It is always open and anticipatory. The text does not possess some absolute meaning which inheres self-sufficiently within itself. The meaning only comes into being through the process of understanding.

A person wishing to understand a text places him or herself immediately in a dialogic situation involving a question and answer process. 'Prejudices' or foresights are an essential part of this activity, for the answers one gets from the text are, in effect, only as good as the questions one asks of it and asking questions is not a value-free process. An essential starting point is to dispel prejudices against prejudice (1975: 240) and to distinguish between legitimate and illegitimate prejudices through a dialogic interrogation in which the truth of the other is allowed to assert itself. A false dialogue in understanding the past is one which is one-sided, elevating either the subject or the object of knowledge. The interpreter must use his or her prejudices to understand 'otherness' while remaining open to learn from what is being studied.

> A person who seeks to understand must question what lies behind what is said. He must understand it as an answer to a question. If we go back behind what is said, then we inevitably ask questions beyond what is said. We understand the sense of the text only by acquiring the horizon of the question that, as such, necessarily includes other possible answers. ... The logic of the human sciences is ... a logic of the question.
>
> (Gadamer 1975: 333)

Gadamer's model of understanding is like a conversation between persons rather than something erected on immovable solid foundations which, right from the start, enable us to dismiss the conversation of the 'other' as nonsense: 'The meaning of a text is not to be compared with an immovably and obstinately fixed point of view which suggests only one question to the person who is trying to understand it ... a "fusion of horizons" ... is the full realisation of conversation, in which something is expressed that is not only mine or my author's but common' (1975: 350).

The hermeneutic circle involves a logic of understanding in which one starts with a set of prejudices with regard to the meaning of the text to be understood. We cannot understand a text or an alien culture unless we make guesses about its form and nature. These in effect allow us to pose questions to the text or the culture in question. The main problem is to find the question to which the text provides answers. The answers modify the initial set of prejudices, allowing a fresh set of questions to be posed, and so on. For this process to be successful the investigator must be prepared to be told something. He or she must be sensitive to the text's newness and difference. Such a sensitivity, rather than requiring extinction of the self or a neutrality or indifference to that being studied, requires a conscious process involving the assimilation of one's own fore-meanings and prejudices (Gadamer 1975: 238). Gadamer insists that the text is not simply to be understood in terms of authorial intentions; it is inevitably read in different circumstances, which entail that understanding is a productive process. It does not attempt to produce a simulacrum. We examine a text not in terms of authorial intention but in relation to the subject matter contained within it, to which we respond with our own words.

Gadamer proposes, then, a form of dialogic understanding of 'otherness' involving a continuous process of question and answer. When this process proceeds far enough the end result is a fusion of horizons between the interpreter and the text, the past and the present, which retains fidelity to neither. Something new is produced. The problem becomes: How do we know when this fusion of horizons takes place? Why should the horizons fuse at all? Is the model of the conversational dialogue grounded in tradition appropriate to understand this process?

TEXTUAL DISTANCIATION

For Ricoeur (1981) the meaning of the sentence takes on a material character according to the wider discursive formation (arena of writing/speaking) in which it is situated, so that the same sentence and the same words can take on different meanings in relation to the social conditions of their enunciation and reception. While the sign is to be defined in its difference, the sentence in which it occurs is endowed with reference. Discourse is a medium through which *langue* is transcended, something which grasps and takes hold of the world, the self and others. The significance of polysemy can only be adequately grasped through a consideration of the individual sentences making up written discourses. Each of these refers to others and helps to create the overall 'meaning effect' of the text. The sentences, when taken together, both actively constitute and simultaneously embody a surplus of meaning.

In analysing language we move from considering it (1) as a system of signs to (2) in terms of types of sentences to (3) as sequences of these sentences in texts. For Ricoeur the sentence is the basic unit of discourse and when we move from the sentence to the text we move from semantics to hermeneutics. The text is a structured totality which is irreducible to the sentences of which it is made up. We cannot understand the text simply by breaking it down into sentences or signs within these sentences. In other words the text has a holistic character. It is something much more than its component parts. Language is not a mere medium but something worked upon to impose a material form on the world. Ricoeur refers to a four-fold distanciation of the text.

First, the text fixes meaning in a material form. It therefore takes on a different character from the ephemerality of speech in a process of 'intentional exteriorization', providing an archive for individual and collective memory (Ricoeur 1981: 147). Austin (1962) and Searle (1969) break down spoken language into a hierarchy of acts distributed on three levels: (a) the locutionary or propositional act: the act *of* saying; (b) the level of the illocutionary act: what is done *in* saying – the force of the speech act; and (c) the level of the perlocutionary act: what is done *by the fact* that we speak. The spoken words 'switch off the light' relate an action predicate 'switch off' to a subject and an object: a person and the light. This is the act of saying, which in this case is spoken with the force of an order (the illocutionary act) which may stimulate in the person so ordered pleasure and satisfaction or fear and discomfort: the perlocutionary act. These three components of speech acts are all related by Ricoeur (1981: 135) to the level of the sentence. The locutionary act is exteriorized in the sentence as a proposition with a meaning. The illocutionary act is exteriorized by means of grammatical paradigms 'marking' and investing the force of a sentence. The perlocutionary act Ricoeur refers to as 'discourse *qua* stimulus' – the effects the sentence has on the reader (1981: 135).

Second, the text is distanced from the intentions of its author. Its meanings go beyond these intentions and cannot be conceived solely in terms of them. The 'world' of the text explodes the world of the author, opening itself out to an unlimited series of readings, themselves to be related to the sociohistorical conditions in which the text is read. Although the text fixes meaning in relation to spoken language, this fixing is opened out through the material endurance of the text so that the meaning produced goes far beyond what was meant or intended by the author.

Third, the meaning of the text goes beyond the social conditions of its production. It can, potentially, be read by anyone capable of reading and is addressed to an audience whose boundaries remain unknown.

> In contrast to the dialogical situation where the *vis à vis* is determined by the very situation of discourse, written discourse creates an audience which extends in principle to anyone who can read. The freeing of the written material with respect to the dialogical condition of discourse is the most significant effect of writing. It implies that the relation between writing and reading is no longer a particular case of the relation between speaking and hearing.
>
> (1981: 139)

So the text in effect decontextualizes itself from the conditions in which it was produced. Speech, on the other hand, cannot be thought of in this manner: it is very much to be related to a dialogical situation taking place at a particular time and in a particular place.

Fourth, the text is not situated in relation to ostensive references which occur in a dialogic situation. In the latter a failure to understand a speech act can lead to a series of questions and answers capable of clarifying the intention of the speaker supplemented by gestures, tone of voice, pointing, etc. These are all, of course, absent from the text.

Ricoeur argues that social action can be read as a text (1981: Chapter 8) and shares these features of distanciation. Action fixes or objectifies the self's relation to the world and bears a series of resemblances to speech acts. For example, actions exhibit a variety of 'illocutionary traits' and can be interpreted in terms of specific meanings such as expressions of anger, solidarity, affection, etc. Actions, like texts, have consequences which go beyond themselves. Just as we cannot pin the text down to what the author meant to say, actions have unintended as well as intended consequences. Social action, like a text, is open to the interpretation of anyone who watches ('reads') it. Actions may have consequences going far beyond the initial contexts in which they take place and their interpretation must therefore transcend the social conditions in which actions are produced. Actions, for Ricoeur, are to be interpreted in precisely the same manner as texts.

The main problem with this position is that actions, because they are physical, living, human *events*, simply cannot be decontextualized or distanciated from the social conditions of their production in the manner of texts. Ricoeur's extension of his argument of four-fold distanciation from text to social action runs into serious difficulty but if we extend it in relation to material culture such a difficulty does not seem to arise. We can readily understand that material culture fixes meaning. It can be understood to embody 'illocutionary' and 'perlocutionary' forces in relation to agents. It is an objectification of a subject's relation to the world. Material culture establishes certain 'propositions', which do something in the world and affect people's actions. Its meaning goes beyond what-ever intentions the individual artisan may have had. Once produced, it becomes decontextualized from the conditions of its production and ostensive reference.

HERMENEUTIC UNDERSTANDING, STRUCTURAL ANALYSIS

If for Ricoeur the text embodies a four-fold distanciation, then it follows that for him, as for Gadamer, it has a plurivocal nature. We decide between different interpretations according to rational debate and argument through which we may hope to reach agreement. This is a matter of probability rather than certainty. Understanding is a process in which we appropriate meaning and which involves a struggle against cultural or temporal distance and a battle against the estrangement of the interpreter from meaning. Interpretation '"brings together", "equalizes", renders "contemporary and similar"', thus genuinely making one's *own* what was initially *alien*' (Ricoeur 1981: 159). In order to reach an adequate understanding it is necessary to proceed from the surfaces of a text to its depths and guard against examining it superficially. It is here that Ricoeur usefully links a structural analysis with hermeneutics.

In a number of important texts Ricoeur has set out elements of a critique of structuralism and attempted to integrate a structuralist methodology within a wider hermeneutic philosophical tradition (Ricoeur 1974: Section 1; 1981: Chapter 5). Ricoeur argues that what occurs in Lévi-Strauss' work in particular is an illegitimate extension of structuralism from a methodological series of opera-tions into a philosophy. The putative solution is a structural hermeneutics. The major problems with a structuralist or a semiotic position as exemplified in Barthes' *Elements of Semiology* (1984) discussed above are:

1 A lack of self-reflexivity. Structuralism puts everything at a distance and asserts a subject–object dichotomy. It separates the person doing the investigation from that being investigated. In so doing it establishes a non-historical relationship between subject and object: 'understanding is not seen here as the recovery of meaning ... there is no hermeneutic circle ... no historicity to the relation of understanding' (Ricoeur 1974: 33–4). There is little reflection on the origins of the theories nor any attempt to relate them to the sets of historical and social circumstances in which they arise.

2 Diachrony is subordinated to synchrony. Within Ricoeur's hermeneutics the inverse holds true: diachrony is only meaningful through its relation to synchrony. The major point of contention is that of the relation of structure to historical event and for Ricoeur the latter must be primary. History – diachrony – is not simply a passage from one structural synchronic state to another, but involves human praxis. Humanity constructs itself through linguistic and other productions.

3 Many of these problems arise from the use of a Saussurian linguistic model in which there is a systematic neglect of the act of situated speech (discourse). Ricoeur poses a rhetorical question:

> Would it not be just as much in keeping with the teachings of linguistics if one held that language, and all the mediations for which it serves as a model, was the unconscious instrument by means of which a speaking subject can attempt to understand being, beings, and himself?
>
> (1974: 54)

What structuralism and semiotics do not take into account is language as a medium for expression and self-reflection. Although the act of speaking is structurally determined by an unconscious grammar, people speak with a purpose: they wish to make statements about something. Humanity speaks in order to be able to *say* (1974: 84). For Ricoeur the understanding of myth or any other meaning tradition must take place through the conscious appropriation of symbolic content by an active interpreter entering directly into the semantic field of that which is to be understood. To do this one inevitably enters an hermeneutic circle involving a productive dialogue with the 'other'. In any structural or semiotic study the apprehension of similitude or homologies between different systems, e.g. rules 'generating' burial practices, culinary practices and pot designs or, in the case in hand, rock carvings, is a matter of an hermeneutic process of active appropriation of the content of the 'other'. Hermeneutics fills a gap or radical lack in structuralism. It clothes structuralism in more viable philosophical trappings.

If hermeneutics fills or supplies a lack in structuralism then for Ricoeur the reverse is also true – structuralism extends hermeneutics in a fresh direction. The relationship between the two is complementary rather than antagonistic, as long as structuralism is understood as a productive methodology inhering within an hermeneutic philosophy. A structuralist and semiotic position simply exposes structural form from 'within' that being studied but interpretation for Ricoeur requires a form of active appropriation on the part of the interpreting subject. It relates that studied to the self. Interpretation overcomes distance. What a structuralist analysis does with singular power is to impugn the surface semantics of cultural texts to reveal a depth semantics which is simultaneously the real living semantics. Structural analysis, then, represents a vital stage between a naive and a critical interpretation, between a superficial understanding and a depth interpretation. Explanation and interpretation take place along an 'hermeneutical arc', integrating and linking them together (Ricoeur 1981: 161). Gone, then, are any claims to an independent existence for structuralism as a fundamentally different form of philosophy. Instead it forms an invaluable tool in the hermeneutic grasping and appropriation of experience, channelled back into the concerns of the self. Structuralism constitutes one moment in a much wider process, the apex of an arc that begins with the self, leads to an in-depth constitution and appropriation of the 'other', finally returning to the self a fresh plenitude of meaning.

THE ROLE OF METAPHOR: DIGITAL LOGIC, ANALOGIC LOGIC

Ricoeur stresses the central importance of metaphor in interpretation and understanding (1981: Chapter 6). The metaphorical meaning of a word cannot be found in any dictionary. Metaphorical meaning is opposed to literal meaning. It is something more than an actualization of one of the possible meanings of a word. Metaphor works by transforming an actual or attributed property into one of the senses in which the word is to be understood, not only by actualizing a potential connotation but by establishing it as a stable one. Metaphor opens out the possibility that some of the properties of an object may be given a new status and meaning in language. Ricoeur notes that 'to speak of properties of *things* (or *objects*), which are supposed not yet to have been signified, is to admit that new, emergent meaning is not drawn from anywhere, at least not from anywhere in language (*the property is an implication of things, not of words*)' (1981: 173–4, my emphasis). This is an absolutely crucial argument that can lead us away from a 'digital' structuralist or semiotic logic based on the assumption of an isomorphism between linguistic meaning and meaning in material culture to a position in which the materiality of the object world is recognized as not being reducible to language, and residing in a metaphorical or 'analogic' logic. This requires further exploration.

Much of the discussion so far in this book has more or less assumed that a structural and semiological understanding of material culture based on a general analogy with language can adequately capture its form and nature. However, it needs to be remembered that, if I could capture and express *everything* in a painting in words, *everything* in a pot design, *everything* in a piece of music and so on, these material forms would be completely redundant. There would be no point in listening to the music, looking at the painting or the pot. Barth (1975: 157) has specifically suggested that the analogy with language based primarily on a conception of difference and binary oppositions, as found in the work of Lévi-Strauss, needs to be transcended if we are to grasp the nature of the signifying power of material culture. We cannot simply assume the existence of a single code for ritual, pot designs, etc. in which messages are uniformly cast nor can we assume that homologies exist between different symbolic systems such that they can be regarded as transformations of each other, displaying the same underlying generative logic:

> the meanings of an idiom [symbolic form] derive not from the contrast with the meanings of other idioms in a subsystem. . . . Rather each idiom is employed because of its inherent aptness as a metaphor or analogue. As such, each idiom draws on a wide field of connotations, peculiar to itself and different for each idiom in the sub-set.
>
> (Barth 1975: 161)

This is not to deny that general relations of difference or contrast exist but that these relations of difference and opposition can adequately explain why particular material symbols are utilized in specific ways. Difference and contrast provide one entry into meaning but it is unhelpful to reduce signification to contrast within an overall system. Meaning does not simply depend on difference, and different aspects of the meanings of specific symbols may not be contrastive with everything else. An analogic logic, we might say, depends on a digital contrastive logic for part of its force and potency but cannot be reduced to this level. For Barth part of the potency of material symbols derives from their analogic or metaphorical qualities, through which something familiar or distinctive is used as a model or analogy for something less obvious. In a metaphoric logic there is an inherent connection between form and meaning. Questions of meaning and those concerned with why a certain object is used to signify something are intimately bound together. This is not an entirely arbitrary process. From the perspective of a linguistic analogy or digital logic, man is man because man is not woman, pig, dog, goat, etc. From the perspective of a metaphorical logic the vehicle for conceptualization will be a transformation of that which it conceptualizes or means. Meaning may thus arise independently from any total code. The power of a metaphoric logic is to use imagery from one domain to illuminate relationships in a different one as aids for understanding and conceptualization.

Let us consider some examples. For the Ndembu the milk tree, oozing a white fluid, stands for women's breasts at a grossly physical level, and builds up significative associations involving motherhood, female novices in initiation rites, the principle of matriliny, a specific matrilineage, knowledge, and the unity and persistence of Ndembu society (Turner 1967: 28). But its choice is not entirely arbitrary: there is an obvious resemblance between the white fluids in the growing tree and mothers' milk. Building on this resemblance, a whole significative series is produced. We move from a denotative level to a connotative level of signification but the metaphors are built up by abstracting from the properties of an object, in this case the milk tree, in the world. They do not arise purely from the free-floating productivity of language.

Among the Baktaman and other groups in highland Papua New Guinea the cassowary feather is utilized as an emblem of senior men. The cassowary, a black, bipedal jungle 'ostrich', is the second largest animal known to the Baktaman. It is unique in a fauna of animals which hide rather than run; it makes a habit of eating the sacred, phallic-shaped pandanus fruit. As Barth states, what better image could one adopt (Barth 1975: 160)?

The point is that material signs are frequently of this nature – abstracting and building on properties of the natural and physical world in order to map and relate these features in terms of the social, but it is important to avoid any simplistic one-to-one correlation between the concrete properties of a symbol and its connotative meanings. Meaning does not just reflect; it is also produced, contrived. In other words, meaning arises from operations performed on things. To take another example from the Baktaman: soil is (i) polluting as something to live in – animals of the soil are impure, while animals of the air are the purest of all; (ii) a sign of grief – you dirty yourself with the soil; (iii) a sign of festivity when applied to the chest in patterns; (iv) neither clean nor unclean when used for hearths; (v) fertile – in the gardens it gives growth to taro and must not be polluted by semen from incest; (vi) used to bless the areas where pigs sleep (white soil) (Barth 1975: 158). It is necessary to assert against some more extreme 'post-structuralist' positions that meaning, especially in relation to material culture, is not endlessly free-flowing. It becomes relatively fixed according to social context and according to the purposes to which it is directed. If meaning were not relatively fixed and stabilized it would no longer be meaningful.

'FUSING' HORIZONS: ETHNOHISTORICAL PERSPECTIVES

With this hermeneutic armoury let us now return to Nämforsen and attempt to read the carvings in a fresh way. One obvious and well-tried approach to fusing horizons, gaining an entry point into meaning, is to use generalized anthropological principles and/or direct ethnohistorical evidence. Helskog (1987) has specifically suggested that there may exist a long-term continuity between the depictions on the rock carvings in northern Scandinavia which ceased to be produced towards the beginning of the early Iron Age (c. 500 BC) and those found on the membranes of historically documented Saami shamans' drums from the seventeenth to the nineteenth centuries. These drums were used by patriarchal family heads and shamans specializing in divination, sacrifice and ritual curing, aided through establishing contact with the spirit world. There are a few depictions of drums on the rock carvings at Alta and this, together with the occurrence of a range of motifs depicting human and animal forms and occasionally boats on the Saami drums, leads Helskog to suggest a long-term continuity in shamanistic ritual practices and prehistoric depictions.

The possibility that drums and shamans existed in prehistory, and the knowledge that drums were a commonly used instrument among the Saami in early pre-Christian history, indicates that the use of the depictions in connection with rituals might have a long tradition in northern Scandinavia. This tradition existed 6,000 years ago, and is probably represented in its last stage by the drums and their associated rituals.

(Helskog 1987: 30)

Helskog's analysis might have been strengthened somewhat by considering design field structure and interrelationships rather than the presence/absence of particular motifs. Even in the analyses he does undertake, however, he notes major differences: the Alta rock carvings are dominated by reindeer, the drums by human figures, some of which are identifiable as gods and spirits. This difference between an essentially animal art and an art on the drums depicting mainly people and cultural objects (e.g. tents; various types of more abstract symbols) would appear to be of great significance and the claims regarding a 6,000-year shamanistic tradition rather thin.

With regard to the specific details of the rock carvings at Nämforsen, the development of a putative link with Saami ethnohistorical data is likely to be useless. Reindeer do not appear on the carving surfaces; nor do drums. The natural environment is one dominated by coniferous forest rather than tundra. The bear was an animal of central ritual importance in the context of Saami shamanism (Edsman 1965; Bäckman and Hultkrantz 1978: 82ff.) and again is absent at Nämforsen, while there appears to be no body of Saami myths concerned with the elk. Lindqvist has made the interesting suggestion that the historically documented bear cult may have superseded an earlier emphasis on the elk documented in the widespread occurrence of elk-head sculptures in northern Scandinavia and Siberia and in the rock carvings (Lindqvist 1978: 19). However, local differences need to be taken into account and there is a very real danger in pursuing sweeping generalizations with regard to such a vast geographical area. Carpelan (1975) has documented the widespread prehistoric occurrence of elk-head *and* bear-head sculptures. Northern Norwegian rock art contrasts with the northern Swedish material in the presence of bear depictions.

What is even more surprising is that, within Swedish folklore and myth taken as a whole, there is an almost total absence of reference to the elk. Brief notes, useless for my purposes, and generally displaying complete ignorance of the animal (e.g. the elk was reputed to have such stiff legs it slept leaning against a tree and once on the ground could not get up; a good hunting method was therefore to make notches in the tree the elk slept against so it would fall over!) are recorded by Berg (1978) and Tillhagen (1985). This situation contrasts with copious myths concerned with other animals (Szabó, personal communication). This may be because the elk was over-hunted for a long period from the seventeenth century onwards. The large elk population that exists today is a relatively recent historical phenomenon.

Hultkrantz has noted, in a general way, a point of considerable significance: a 'magic and ritual distinction between land and water, and animals of land and water [is] found in Finno-Ugric and Eskimo religions' (Hultkrantz 1965: 296–7) and this can be followed up by considering a large body of ethnohistorical material recorded by Russian ethnographers working mainly during the 1920s and the 1930s among Evenk hunter-fisher-gatherer groups from the taiga belt of western Siberia (Michael 1963). Here the natural environment, although harsher in winter, is similar to that at Nämforsen, i.e. forest dominated by a similar flora and fauna, criss-crossed by large and often turbulent rivers. Field-work was carried out among the Evenk groups before their incorporation within the Soviet socialist state. Anisimov states that

> Before the Russians came to Siberia at the beginning of the 17th century, the small tribes of the contemporary peoples of the North were at a stage of primitive clan society. Tsarist colonial policy helped to preserve this backwardness ... as a result of which they continued to preserve, down to the Soviet era, many characteristic features of primitive communal structure. Some of them nomadized over the broad expanses of the taiga and tundra, occupied in hunting and reindeer breeding; others lived a seminomadic life along the banks of Siberian rivers and along the shores of the seas, fishing and hunting.
>
> (Anisimov 1963a: 158–9)

Vasilevich (1963), Anisimov (1963a, 1963b) and others from whom they draw some of their information make a very strong argument for regarding shamanism, practised among the Evenks in a manner somewhat analogous to the Saami, as a relatively late development incorporating an earlier set of totemic beliefs. They take an orthodox Marxist line following the work of Engels (1884), who embraced the evolutionary framework set out by Morgan (1871, 1877), arguing that a totemic view of the universe, subsequently modified by shamanism, was originally an ideological projection of a matriarchal clan society. These arguments about an originary matriarchy, based on early ethnographic work on Australian Aboriginal kinship systems, appear to be unnecessary but the general point that a ritual and cosmological system involving shamanism can in northern Eurasia be regarded as a partial transformation of an earlier totemic system is a forceful one. Indeed, it can be suggested that the time when rock carvings cease to be produced in northern Scandinavia signals a change from totemism to shamanism. In the context of the new system the older rock carvings cease to have any meaning.

Put very broadly, the major contrasts between totemism and shamanism can be summarized as a contrast between the mapping of social differences in terms of perceived differentiation in the natural world and a system in which an individual (the shaman) mediates between the social and the supernatural on behalf of the group. In a shamanistic ritual system social differences are no longer based on a link with natural categories, and the link with the supernatural shifts from the collective to the individual level, from the social group to the shaman. It is the shaman who summons up ancestor spirits to aid him (shamanism is a male prerogative) and these are the individualized ancestor spirits of the shaman rather than being generalized to the group as a whole. Totemic progenitors, usually conceived as half-human, half-animal, become transformed into the ancestors or spirit helpers of the shaman, clan rivers become shaman's rivers and so on. Power, based on mediation with the spirit world, becomes individualized rather than a collective possession of the group.

Such transformations can be clearly seen in Evenk concepts surrounding shamanism and the spirit world, the symbolic structure of the shaman's tent, the shaman's clothing and the form of shamanistic ceremonies in all of which there is a systematic tension between the individual and the collective and in the relationship between the natural and the supernatural. For example, the shaman's ritual tent is erected and furnished collectively, the ceremonies that take place in and around it involve the entire clan and connected with them are concepts of the rebirth of nature. Clan members have the right to use shamanistic equipment during the ceremonies and an obligation to enter into shamanistic activity. However, as soon as the shaman's equipment is put into his hands, it becomes untouchable by others.

> This is motivated by the fact that the shaman, having taken the shamanistic equipment into his hands, plants in it his own spirit helpers, who are subject only to him, and who chastise the person who, not being a shaman, that is, not possessing the supernatural qualities proper to the shaman, dares to conduct shamanistic activity with the help of this equipment. ... The fact that the first part of the rites is carried out by all the clansmen and the second by the shaman only shows no less clearly that the clan rites which preceded shamanism were the affair of the whole clan.
>
> (Anisimov 1963b: 116–17)

In a similar manner the shaman's clothing and equipment is a curious *bricolage* of elements derived from natural and military metaphoric transformations: his drum is thought of as an animal (a wild deer), alternatively as his boat and his weapon. His robe is an animal (wild deer, elk, bear) or a bird (eagle) and is his armour (1963b: 118). Rather than pursue these putative totemic transformations further and attempt to sort out an originary set of transformed elements, an undertaking fraught with difficulties, I now wish to turn to consider some fundamental Evenk cosmological concepts within the context of Evenk shamanism as documented by Anisimov (1963a, 1963b) and Vasilevich (1963).

THE COSMIC RIVER AS A LINK BETWEEN THREE WORLDS

Among the Evenks the universe is divided into three worlds, an upper, a middle and a lower world. These are sometimes represented as three circles and all these worlds are duplicates of each other. The middle world is the earth on which humanity resides, the upper world associated with controlling spirits and the lower world, in a large number of myths, with the dead. The world is rendered in all dialects as *buga* or *dunne* meaning undifferentiated nature. Humans entering either the upper or lower worlds remain invisible to the inhabitants. In some myths the entrance to the upper world may be attained through entering an opening in the sky, commonly associated with the north star, which is intimately linked with the constellation of the Great Bear. The Great Bear is called *kheglun* by almost all Evenks, in a few dialects *ataktak*, meaning in all cases elk (Vasilevich 1963: 50). There are numerous creation myths explaining the origin of *kheglun* in terms of a cosmic hunt. One mythic variant relates:

> One day the hero Chakiptylan wished to kill the heavenly elk. He gave chase and loosed an animal which fell at the feet of the elk. *Eksheri*, the master spirit of the upper world, stopped him because he had wished to kill the heavenly elk – and caused him to rot in his place. Four stars of the constellation are the elk, three are his shadow, and the little star near the right of the lower one is Chakiptylan's arrow.
>
> (Vasilevich 1963: 50)

But the significance of the elk goes far beyond an association with the Great Bear constellation. The upper world or *ugu bugu* was inhabited by powerful or supreme spirits, masters of all the phenomena of the natural world – the taiga, animals and humans. As duplicate of the middle world inhabited by humans, the visible blue sky becomes the taiga of the upper world and it is inhabited by the cosmic elk. Anisimov states that

> During the day the elk goes into the thickets of the heavenly taiga, and therefore is not visible from the land of the people. At night he comes out onto the mountain peaks, and being the most powerful of the dwellers (stars) in heaven, may be seen by people from the earth. Judging by the fact that the constellation Little Bear is considered in these concepts as kheglun's calf, we may conclude that the cosmic image of the elk is understood at the same time as that of a 'mother-elk'.
>
> (Anisimov 1963a: 162)

The myths, then, relate cosmic hunts of a female elk in the heavenly taiga. This is also related to the sun cycle, day and night, warmth and cold. In some myths the heavenly elk, pursued by a hunter, frequently conceived as a bear, carries off the sun into the thicket of the taiga, transforming day into night. The elk is also associated with the passage of the seasons, chased by hunters across the three worlds of the universe until finally killed in the taiga of the upper world. The elk then comes to life once more and with it the whole of nature: the ice breaks up, the earth is freed from snow, fresh green appears on the taiga, migratory birds appear and animals breed (1963a: 163). The importance of the elk is evident not only in the myths but in ritual practices, rites of regeneration and revival, and is centrally associated with shamanistic ceremonies. While primarily belonging to the upper world, elk imagery also occurs in a transformed state in the lower world in the form of the guardian, *Kalir*, the mythical deer of the lower world, represented as having the antlers of an elk and the tail of a fish.

The *khargi* are spirit ancestors associated both with the shamans (i.e. ancestors of the shamans) and spirit rulers of the underworld. As already mentioned, they are often associated with rapids and whirlpools as doors or thresholds to this underworld. These *khargi* are beings of a dual nature, half-human, half-animal. They perform a cycle of transformation: being transformed into a shaman's spirit as an animal-double of the shaman, they enter the middle world from the world of the ancestors. On a shaman's death they revert to the form of an animal. Anisimov notes that the birth and death of the shaman were conceived in the form of 'topogentilic' concepts embodying concepts of the mother animal, a maternal place of birth-giving, in turn linked with the shaman's world tree, *turu* (Anisimov 1963a: 166).

The three worlds are connected by the shaman's or clan river, *engdekit*. The upper world is the place of the souls of both people and animals, where the cosmic river has its swampy headwaters (*detur*), rich with lush pastures. *Det* signifies swamp, tundra, mossy glade in the taiga: favoured pasturage for the elk. In the mythologies of the Selkup Evenks the cosmic swamp gives rise to two rivers which flow parallel to one another before joining at the point at which they enter the underworld (Anisimov 1963a: 188). The cosmic river is long, with great rapids variously referred to as *kultyr* (threshold) or *urkel* (doors). In some myths there are seven, in others nine rapids, the last being the most terrifying, and beyond this the river's mouth, entrance to the underworld through which the lower part of the *engdekit* flows. This entrance is guarded by spirits preventing the dead from moving out from the underworld. The *engdekit* has a number of tributaries or shamans' rivers along which the shamans' spirit helpers or *khargi* live. Whirlpools in rivers on earth provide entrances to the shamans' rivers and the shamans may be either benevolent or dangerous, according to which group of people they help. Their spirit helpers are engaged in a constant battle:

These spirits help their shamans during shamanistic perfor-
mances, and the rest of the time they keep up a constant fight
with the helper spirits of enemy shamans. The fight is carried
on by not allowing enemy spirits to do unpleasant things to
the people served by their shaman, while on the other hand
trying themselves to bring troubles to the people protected by
the enemy shaman. ... Believing this, the Evenks were often
afraid of strong and noisy whirlpools. The spirits of enemy
shamans always looked for the chance to pull one through a
whirlpool into *engdekit*.

(Vasilevich 1963: 58)

The *engdekit* was interpreted by different groups and shamans
among the Evenks as:

1 A shamanistic road-river. Every clan must have its shaman, each
  one with his special road to the other worlds of the universe along
  this river. The river becomes associated with the shamans and is a
  place of prohibition for others.
2 A clan river common to all shamans of the clan and kinsmen.
3 The concept of two parallel flowing courses of the river is linked
  in some groups to a dual moiety organization, with shamans from
  different groups making their way to the upper or lower worlds
  along the two river channels (Anisimov 1963a: 188).

Common to all the Evenks is the importance of this dangerous
river full of rapids linking the three worlds of the universe and the
importance of whirlpools or 'entrances' in it. This river is variously
conceived as running either north to east or east to west. The
engdekit empties into the lower world, entering a 'sea of the
deceased'. The spirit of the sea is conceived as an old man (Anisimov
1963a: 180). This view of the sea of the underworld being controlled
by a mythical male master contrasts with the view of the upper
world as having a female spirit (an old woman) as the chief deity
(1963a: 168). This can be represented in a series of related transformations as:

upper world : lower world
(heavenly taiga) : (sea of the deceased)
land : water
old woman : old man
female : male

THE SHAMAN'S TENT

The course of the cosmic river on an east–west axis becomes symbolized in the construction of the shaman's ritual tent, which was divided into three parts: an internal area and two galleries, *darpe* and *onang*. The *darpe* was always orientated to the east of the tent entrance and the *onang* to the west. The circle of ground in the middle occupied by the tent symbolized both the middle world and the shaman's island in the middle of the clan river (Anisimov 1963b: 86–7). In the centre of the tent was placed the shaman's *turu*, a young larch tree. The *turu* also connects the three worlds. In various rites and myths it performs a similar role to the *engdekit*. The *turu* may grow between the three worlds with its roots in the lower world, trunk in the middle world, and crown in the sky. According to Evenk shamans, each possesses a clan *turu* represented as a larch tree, to which not only the shaman's life, but the life of the entire clan is linked: 'the link was conceived as direct and was identified with the image of the mythical mother-animal, venerated as the chief of the spirits of the clan as well as of the Shaman's *turu*' (Anisimov 1963a: 182). Additionally each shaman had a lower, middle and upper *turu*. The lower *turu* was linked with the dwelling place of the shaman's spirit half-human, half-animal ancestors. In the middle world the shaman's *turu* holds their external soul, i.e. the animal-double or *khargi* which comes to the shaman during ceremonies and then returns to the tree. In the upper world clouds and luminous bodies are found on the *turu*.

The shaman sat on a raft made of wooden images of salmon trout spirits. In the *darpe*, symbolizing the route to the upper world, stood representations of giant wild reindeer and fish spirits (salmon, pike) swimming in the upper river and guarding the clan's storehouse of souls. In the *onang*, entrance to the lower world, were spirit-larches, numerous bird figures and a large figure of the mythical shamanistic elk (Anisimov 1963b: 88–93). The major oppositional elements of the structure can be represented as in Figure 48.

The shaman on his island or raft of fish spirits mediates with his *khargi* in the lower world. The shamanistic trance associated with this act of mediation is clearly a liminal state and this also becomes reflected in the shaman's dress. The shaman's robe retains characteristic features of female outer dress and decoration so that, as spiritual mediator, he becomes both male and female just as his spirit helpers are both human and animal.

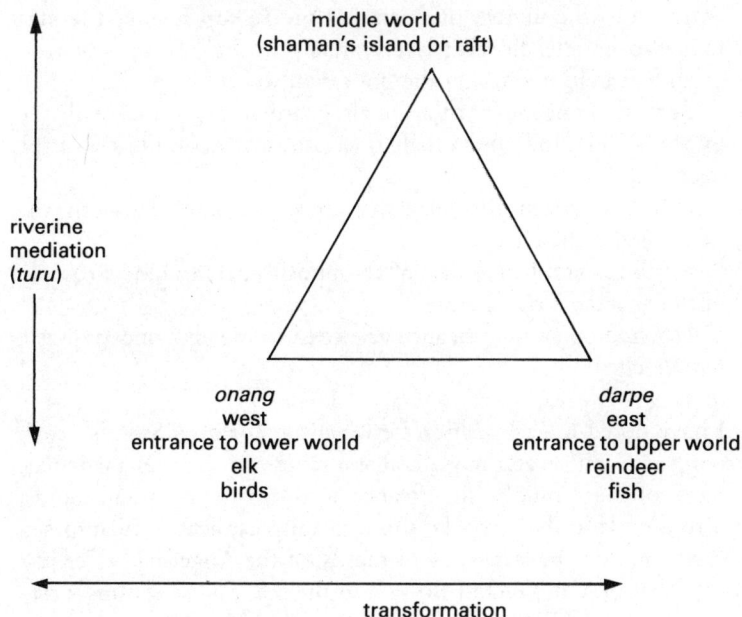

Figure 48 Representation of the elements of the shaman's tent

NÄMFORSEN IN THE LIGHT OF EVENK COSMOLOGY

A number of features of the Evenk cosmological system provide a powerful series of parallels with discussions of the location of the northern Swedish rock art sites and interpretations of the designs that have already been undertaken solely on the basis of the archaeological evidence:

1 The importance of rivers in the cosmological system and their link with specific clans;
2 The notion of a cosmic river flowing from east to west and mediating between the different worlds of the cosmos, and the conception of rapids as providing openings to these other worlds;
3 The liminal symbolism associated with the shaman's island in the cosmic river;
4 The idea that the point at which the cosmic river flows into the sea is marked by the most violent series of rapids marking the

135

entrance to the underworld; among the Selkup Evenks the idea
that two parallel flowing rivers arising in the heavens meet on
earth just before entering the underworld;

5 A dualistic conception of a female guardian associated with the
upper world (land) and a male one associated with the sea of the
deceased;

6 The link between the shaman's *turu* (mediator between the
worlds) and the elk;

7 Use of birds and fish as part of an oppositional meaning structure
in the shaman's ritual tent;

8 The cosmological significance accorded to the elk conceived as a
female elk.

I have noted the association between the northern Swedish rock
carving sites with water in general and rapids on rivers in particular.
In view of the symbolic significance accorded to rivers and rapids,
and to islands in these rapids, this is readily explicable. Nämforsen
was situated on the last series of rapids on the Ångerman river just
above the point at which it flows into the sea. The river runs west–
east; just above Nämforsen it consists of two parallel river courses
arising in the mountains (the heavens). The link with Selkup Evenk
mythology is almost exact. The elk heads on poles become explicable, like the river, as symbolic mediators of essential sacred
significance, while the opposition elk: boat :: female: male finds
strong correlation in Evenk mythological structures in which fish
and birds are also emphasized. It now seems possible to suggest that
the Ångerman river played a similar symbolic role in prehistoric
cosmologies as the *engdekit* among the Evenks; that the islands
were central ritual liminal spaces intimately linked with the rapids as
entrance to other worlds but these were collectively utilized rather
than shaman's islands.

The use of ethnohistorical data is, of course, fraught with
difficulties and can only take us further in an hermeneutic appropriation of the meaning of the carvings to a limited degree. We still
need to ask the questions: Of what specifically do these carving
surfaces speak? Is there one message or many? In order to attempt
to answer these questions we can take a rather different direction
which does not necessarily entirely contradict the structural analysis
just undertaken but rather focuses on a different level of meaning.
The starting point here will be to consider in more detail the content
of the designs and their spatial relations at Nämforsen from a

perspective in which the carving surfaces are regarded as constituting part of a much wider mythological and ritual system. The questions then become: Are we witnessing a process of telling stories in pictures? If so, what are the narratives about? Are they coherent or contradictory? Do they shift through time and across space – between the carving pages?

NÄMFORSEN AS A HETEROTOPIA

Virtually all cultures have their utopias – wished-for worlds that do not exist, sites with no place, a perfected world, often an inversion of society as lived. Most cultures also have their heterotopias, real places 'which are something like counter-sites, a kind of effectively enacted utopia in which the real sites, all the other real sites that can be found within the culture, are simultaneously represented, contested, and inverted. Places of this kind are outside of all places, even though it may be possible to indicate their location in reality' (Foucault 1986: 24). In small-scale societies such heterotopias are sacred places often associated with life-crisis rituals and ceremonies, removed from day-to-day existence; the meanings to the social actors using them are typically heterogeneous, and they change through time. They may juxtapose in a single real space other places or spaces to create a perfect ordering of existence, meticulously well-ordered as opposed to messy daily life-spaces. Nämforsen would seem to be such a unique heterotopic place. The very location and the quantity and complexity of the carving surfaces compared to the other sites in northern Sweden indicate this, as do the insights drawn from the ethnohistorical data. The contemporary settlement site, in view of its size, longevity of occupation and peculiar absence of elk or beaver bones, coupled with the evidence for large-scale tool manufacture, suggests a central ritual aggregation site for dispersed groups of hunter-fisher-gatherers using the rock carving area. The absence of elk bones is easily explained in terms of selective deposition. We might well expect the bones of an animal of central cultural importance and totemic value not to be mixed with the bones of other species in a central ritual site. The status of the beaver remains enigmatic – absent in the carved depictions and present in the settlement deposits – a taboo animal at certain locations or seasons?

The rock carvings are removed from the settlement area, situated below it along the river banks and out on the islands. This settlement (see Figure 11) is sited on the southern river bank and although most of the rock carvings in the Nämforsen area face in a southerly direction, i.e. towards the settlement, most or all would not have been clearly visible from it. Painting the motifs would have increased the degree of visibility perhaps but this is a *carving* site. As paint has been preserved at other sites without carvings and there are no traces of paint whatsoever at Nämforsen, we can perhaps conclude that these surfaces never were painted and in this case would have been invisible from the settlement. The rock carvings that do occur along the southern river banks and are easily accessible from the settlement have the following features, which seem to be particularly significant:

(i) They are few in number (Table 1);
(ii) depictions of humanity and shoe soles do not occur;
(iii) complex carving surfaces on which more than three de*sign* types occur are absent (Table 5; Figure 14);
(iv) the majority consist of the repetition of only one or two different de*signs*: double-line boats and/or outline elks;
(v) there is a complete absence of fabulous designs such as double-headed elks or elk–boat transformations. The boats possess only simplified as opposed to naturalistic elk-head prows.

In other words, the depictions appear to be rather prosaic in character. Here we certainly have a display of some structural elements but in contrast to the major carving panels on the islands and on the northern river banks (Figures 13, 15, 16) there do not appear to be any rock carvings which might be interpreted as constituting a visual cosmology or story. The river and the violence of the rapids clearly constitute a boundary which must be crossed between the world of the profane and the world of the sacred. The water is thus a boundary which separates entry to the rock carving areas and must be crossed to reach them on the northern shores and the ritual islands. The island that is most difficult to reach – Brådön – significantly has the most complex carving surface incorporating the circle–cross symbol which is the only one not repeated. No occupation debris has been found on the islands – they were visited rather than occupied. The dangers and trials involved in reaching them would, of course, enhance this quality of being removed from the normal world of social existence.

The rock carvings are situated, then, in a liminal sacred space and it is only in this space that humanity and fabulous creatures are depicted. We can consider each individual carving (e.g. an elk or a boat) as being iconological mythemes which may, on certain carving surfaces, be combined to create visual stories or mythologems. Nämforsen is a mythological site in which elements of the cosmological system are being inscribed in images no doubt serving to objectify in a material form myths about the world and the place of humanity in it. It is necessary, then, to consider in general terms the relationship between oral and visual mythic imagery and that between myth and ritual in order to forge a further hermeneutic point of entry into the meaning of these carvings.

MYTH, RITUAL AND MEANING

Myths establish representations of the world that are not tied down to ordinary experience: in the world of myth almost anything can happen. However, this does not imply that they are unreal. Mythic systems establish meaning and as such relate to reality as lived, to the social construction of the world mediating between individual, collective and cosmogenic experience. Cultures do not have just one myth (except our own – history) but networks of myths that can be related to each other in terms of systems of transformations related to common themes. There may be many transformational variants of the same myth and myths may undergo expansion, deletion or substitution of the meaning units that compose them. Myths may be narrated or graphically inscribed by individuals but their significance resides in the fact that they form part of a collective oral and/or iconographic tradition. Myths may seize on concrete features of the world in a manner analogous to totemic systems – animals, objects, social relations, and construct out of them a logic of the world to make sense of and to order social reality, repetitively ordering and reordering the world using the same limited sets of elements over and over again. Myths are usually expressive rather than abstract and mythical language (whether in words or pictures) operates to produce meaning through a graphic dictionary of images. They unite rather than separate and divide humanity, the world and the cosmos, and any myth may operate simultaneously on a number of planes uniting the geographical, the astronomical, the culinary or alimentary, the technoeconomic, social, political and cosmological aspects of life (Lévi-Strauss 1969). They provide cultural solutions to the world as experienced and may transform, erase or displace contradictions. Myths also provide codes for experience, scenarios for action and meaning, and may ideologically rationalize the social world by establishing, for example, the relative importance of genealogical relations.

Myth typically orders the world by providing sacred reference points or paradigms for action through metaphor. Time and space become plastic and malleable. Simultaneity is created between the present and mythic origins, time becomes collapsed rather than being regarded as a linear series, causes and effects are not separated. The contingencies of the present may be given a sacred quality by integration with an origin lying outside historical time. Myth creates a meaningful history, a *Geschichte* as opposed to chronicle or *historie*.

It seems unhelpful to erect any radical divide between myth and ritual. Rituals are often enacted myth and both act in a similar way to construct experience of the world through a condensation of symbolic structures. Turner (1969) has emphasized the relationship between myth, ritual and liminality. Liminality is that arena of social experience in which new myths and rituals arise. If the state of liminality is contrasted with the ordinary social order in terms of sets of oppositions, a regular set of opposed properties emerges (Turner 1969: 92–3):

Liminality		Normal order
transition	:	state
totality	:	partiality
homogeneity	:	heterogeneity
equality	:	inequality
anonymity	:	systems of nomenclature
absence of status	:	status
nakedness/uniform clothing	:	distinctions of clothing
sexual continence	:	sexuality
minimization of sex distinctions	:	maximization of sex distinctions
absence of rank	:	rank distinctions
no wealth distinctions	:	wealth distinctions
sacredness	:	secularity
sacred instruction	:	technical knowledge
simplicity	:	complexity
heteronomy	:	degrees of autonomy

Liminal ritual states, as opposed to the day-to-day order, become vital components of social reproduction and cosmological orientation and are intimately linked to the telling and re-telling of myth. Myths may be told both in the narrative form of stories or in an iconological form. Here a crucial distinction can be introduced between mythic themes *displaced* into narrative structures and iconological myths or myths created from material symbols which remain relatively *undisplaced*, i.e. the bridging narrative or story links are missing and what we are left with is a set of iconographic mythological symbols without the 'in the beginnings', 'ands', 'therefores' and so on. The elements of the myths remain relatively non-articulated. A verbal displacement of a myth into narrative requires a degree of linearity, inevitably the introduction of a temporal dimension into what may be in essence atemporal. This surreptitious reintroduction of lineal temporality enforced by the narrative form of story-telling can be systematically avoided in iconographical mythical depictions in which linear space–time can be completely collapsed.

I can now return to Nämforsen. I have already argued that the site constitutes a liminal heterotopic space articulating at certain points mythemes into mythologems or visual narratives. It can now be suggested (a) that these iconological mythologems are undisplaced, which will inevitably make it more difficult to understand them than would be the case if Nämforsen were a literary text inscribed into stone; (b) the mythologems should display recognizable liminal properties.

I can now take at least two possible directions, lacking any indigenous informants. The first approach would be to think myself into these undisplaced myths and utilize them as instruments for my own thought. I would be making up various stories and attempting to justify them as a valid accommodation to the iconographic 'facts'. For example, it is interesting to note that elks, humans and boats are all depicted in the same way. What is important is to show the largest surface area: the side of an elk, the side of a boat, people standing with faces forward. At Nämforsen elks and boats may signify not only female and male, the reproduction of the social based on hunting on the one hand and contact and exchange on the other, but also wealth. The more elks and boats depicted the better, because they are the mark of wealth and well-being. Humanity may accumulate wealth but is not responsible for its creation. This depends on the reproduction of elks on the one hand and boats on the other. It is significant that only human reproductive acts and organs are sometimes shown (the phallic men and pregnant women; a sex scene) but not those of elks. There is no direct concern for the reproduction of elks but rather the symbolic reproduction of human society through that of elks and boats. Some of the rock carving surfaces appear to embody variants of creation stories centring on elks and boats, such as one on Notön (Figure 38). Here we see the celestial union of elk with boat, out of which humanity is born: two figures 'float' at the top of the carving surface, another emerges from the boat. This mythologem, then, symbolically illustrates the crucial importance of elks and boats to social reproduction. In such a statement as this, do I overstretch the limits of 'serious' or 'scientific' archaeological discourse (for some I am aware this started with the first sentence of this book!) and enter a fantasy land of my own making? For the present, at least, this is the kind of potentially narcissistic narrative I wish to avoid and will instead consider the rock carvings from another angle.

The second approach is one in which, rather than trying to specify *what* the carvings mean, I instead focus attention on *how* they mean and this is the line I shall adopt, with a focus on liminality, providing an entry point into this *how* of meaning.

At this point it is instructive to consider one of the most complex rock carving surfaces in more detail to provide a further entry into meaning content (Figure 46, p. 108). This is one of the most striking and best-preserved rock carving surfaces at Nämforsen with representations of at least forty-three elks, three humans, two birds, tools, three fish and six boats. The majority of the depictions are scooped out. For the sake of ease of exposition the carving surface will be divided into five subareas (Figure 46: A–E). Three large, single-lined boats provide a partial 'frame' for the carving surface, to the south and west. The two southern boats are provided with magnificent elk heads at either end and have a definite alignment in relation to each other. A number of other features of interest may be noted. The boat to the right, with its scooped-out elk head on the prow, confronts an elk carved in contrasting outline technique. On both boats human crew figures occur and elk heads on upraised poles facing forward in the presumed line of direction of the boat. A further boat to the north has a backward-facing elk head on a pole but lacks clear human figures, although provided with so-called crew strokes that it can be suggested might better be regarded within the context of Nämforsen as phallic representations, suggesting the male qualities of boats in contrast to the female elks. In group E some of the elks are roughly aligned in rows and face right. Below the largest single-line boat are two small double-lined vessels, both facing right and appearing to form part of an integral unit with the elks.

In group A four elks are positioned so as to form an almost interlocking series. To the right of this group is a composite figure with an elk head and body with appended bent human leg. In group B two elks are conjoined with a fish, while in group D angular tools are portrayed along with elks. Group C consists basically of two staggered rows of paired representations. In the lower 'row' two human bodies, one with upturned arms and another with raised pole (and fish?), appear on either side of a pair of elks facing in opposite directions, one above the other. To the right a scooped and an outline elk confront one another with a large angular tool lodged in between. In the upper 'row' two scooped elks face in the same direction, again with an interspersed angular tool. To the left two water birds confront each other. Farther to the left there is a single-lined boat with elk-head terminations and elk-head pole. Above these 'rows' is a series of elks and below them and to the left a salmon is conjoined with the muzzle of an elk.

While most of the elks on this carving surface appear static, some appear to be more active, with bent legs. Some of the elks overlap or conjoin with each other and we have noted two cases of elk–fish conjunction and the opposing outline elk and long, double-lined boat. This carving surface depicts a number of overlapping levels of meaning. First, major motif forms are displayed and paired or grouped, like with like: elks with elks, birds with birds, humans with humans, tools with tools, boats with boats. Identities are thus established. Second, these identities, having been established, are subsequently extended to oppose and simultaneously group different motif forms together. This is a process of establishing relationships and a certain degree of similitude. An obvious linkage between elks and boats is effected (as everywhere else at Nämforsen) through the elk-head prows, but also additionally through the elk heads on upraised poles. Smaller double-lined vessels are directionally grouped with elks and an elk confronts an elk head on a boat. Fish merge with elks and a composite elk–human is depicted. Tools occur in between elks, as do the birds and the human bodies. The latter also appear on the deck lines of the boats. The meaning seems to be that everything is both separate and opposed and yet linked in an overall scheme of things embracing both the cultural and the natural, which are not being distinguished as having separate natures or essences. In other words, boats are as animal-like and alive as elks; the latter are as much a part of human culture as boats. Humanity fits into this ordered series of oppositions and similitudes which represent the order of which it is a physical and conceptual part. Culture and nature are collapsed into each other, integrally linked and mediated within a cosmological symbolic scheme capable of encompassing and conjoining everything.

We can be confident that the carving surfaces at Nämforsen, such as the one just discussed, are before history as we conceive of it, before time and before space (that is to say a chronometric time and a linear space). What we have at Nämforsen is a topological representational space, a space with 'contour' lines that may go up and down, in and out, sometimes almost forming parallel lines, at others contorted into an intricate network of surfaces of overlap and juxtaposition; from lines of elks to a great series of motifs that build on, overlie and complete each other. The circle–cross symbol that I have suggested marks the centre of the carving area, the point at which all the motifs come together (Figure 19), is, quite typically, off-centre.

We also have a series of representations in which time repeats itself: a mythical dream time in which there appears to be little change in the system of representations, only an endlessly repeated series of a limited number of design forms or mythemes. The world is always the same, already complete. It can only be added to, by transforming elements in terms of an iconological logic, over and over again and in exactly the same way.

The carved surfaces are thoroughly ambiguous, and it is this ambiguity that serves to link them together. There is an undivided animal world consisting of elks and ... ? Animals become lumped into one category, fish into another, birds into one more and there are, of course, the human bodies. Everything at Nämforsen is both the same and different and the form of the elk is dominant. Over and over again designs are transformed into others. Birds resemble boats which resemble elks which resemble humans (the elks have only two legs) who carry tools that resemble elk heads which find their correspondence in the form of boat prows. The natural and the cultural remain undifferentiated and both are equally cosmological categories: herds of elks and herds of boats, massive accumulations of animals and huge ships, both of which it is doubtful actually existed.

It is clear that Nämforsen is not just a depiction of the object world. It is rather a visual statement of myths, cosmic categories and associations held to structure both the supernatural world and human existence. The carvings at Nämforsen are not located in the social space of everyday existence but in a ceremonial and cosmo-logical space characterized by unexpected links, strange figures (e.g. the double-headed elks, the elk–humans and elk–boats) and com-plex undisplaced associations. The 'art' is devoted to an ordering of the world based upon associations of similitude and resemblance, in which the form of the elk completely closes the space between nature and culture. Humanity cannot stand apart in the limited interstices of this space but is enveloped as part of the system, one being among others in which no hierarchy of dependence is being indicated. Humanity is merely part of an order which does not fundamentally differentiate between elks and boats and tools or fish, birds, shoe soles and humanity. All are placed alongside each other as integral and linked components in the ordering. A great table of being is created in which humanity, although responsible for the ordering of the carvings, is a subject rather than an object of knowledge. No nature, no culture – rather sets of relations and associations between mythemic elements. There is no hierarchy of categories, with humanity as *representer* of the world at the top, but only series of resemblances and differences. All elks can thus be female and all boats can be male because the terms 'male' and 'female' do not correspond to the natural (sexual differentiation) rather than to the cultural but to an undivided whole embracing both, in which cultural objects, like humans, may have a sex. The taxonomic system employed does not radically distinguish between separate realms of technology or society or nature. Each forms part of and mediates the other. The conception of the human subject and the relationship between people and the world around them is one that is utterly different from the Cartesian cogito of the contem-porary West.

ASPECTS OF LIMINALITY

The world that is being represented – a world dominated by elks and boats – is one in which humanity is thoroughly marginalized, a trace that may appear now and again on carving surfaces but is never isolated and always in association. Humanity may represent the ordering of the world but can never be isolated from this ordering. The social order is, in fact, dependent for its continued existence on this cosmological order. So the coherence of Nämforsen is the creation of an order in which everything has an allotted place. The carving surfaces create order through linking and articulating everything together via a massive system of resemblances and juxtapositions and through allowing elements to touch, overlap and intermingle so that, for example, the extremities of a boat may denote the beginning of an elk. They create both an experience of order and its mode of existence. Culture becomes a mirror of nature which finds its paradigm form in the elk, the geometer of a cosmological practice.

It is possible to recognize in these carvings many of the liminal attributes emphasized by Turner:

(a) Transition and totalization: through a process of establishing resemblances, the different iconological forms are linked together and transform into each other in an ordering of the world able to accommodate everything.
(b) Homogeneity and heteronomy: the elk is structurally linked to all the other design forms.
(c) Equality, absence of status and rank: there is a lack of any hierarchical ordering of motifs on the carving surfaces.
(d) Minimization of sexual differences: the vast majority of human depictions possess an ambiguous sexual status, neither male nor female. Similarly, the elks, lacking antlers, are in a metaphorical sense transitional between a clearly identifiable male or a female state. They are either neuter, like the majority of the humans, or female.
(e) Simplicity: the same designs are employed over and over again.

Nämforsen is not in any sense a mere mirror of the realities of the world for small, scattered hunter-gatherer-fisher bands but more an attempt at an analysis of the ordering of existence and the place of humanity in it. Humanity is both marginal, in a liminal space, and yet has an influence. For example, the passive as opposed to the active elks and the portrayal of elks as body parts in some cases suggests the impact of humans. Both elks and boats have to be moulded to serve human purposes and equally, as nature and culture are undivided, elks and boats have lives of their own. Even if the latter are constructed by humanity, their coming and going (exchange relationships) cannot be controlled by the indigenous hunter-gatherers. A boat on the river or the sea is not fixed but a floating piece of space, sometimes wild and restless according to the state of the waters. Boats, in their very mobility, the fact that they are closed in on themselves, possess metaphorical properties or essences which they share with the movements and habits of elks, largely beyond the control of the local population, and which may be expressed in the carving surfaces as a system of resemblances, intermingling and juxtapositioning.

Although there are definite types of boats, and variations within these types are displayed, it is the elks that provide the fulcrum around which this art is situated, the centre upon which relations are concentrated and from which they become extended in a series of resemblances. However, these resemblances must be at some point counterbalanced by an opposing form and principle which is found in the variation of the boats, the presence of fish, shoe soles and birds, or the whole world would rapidly become reduced to a single form – that of the elk.

The carving surfaces at Nämforsen provide representations of a series of fundamental ideas about social relations, demonstrating how prehistoric modes of thought created relations of similarity and equivalence between what appear to us as fundamentally unlike elements. Systems of relations provided a foundation for and legitimation of economic and social forms and systems of exchange, creating a vast syntax for the world in which each element was linked and conjoined, an imaginary world through which social processes were represented and played out. In this world each element becomes adjusted to another and elks with everything. In this manner meaning is effected through the ordering of the carved rock surfaces. Humanity is a mere trace that operates in this world rather than providing its foundation; all that can be done is to represent the world's cosmological forces by drawing links. In this sense the motif of the shoe sole has a particular resonance (see Figure 29).

Sacred islands, liminality, the symbolic and cosmological integration of scattered hunter-gatherer groups through visual story-telling, and an ontology of the world based on similitude and resemblance revolving around the form of the elk as a life-giving and connective force constitute the essence of Nämforsen. As a central heterotopic ritual site it creates social, cosmological and ontological cohesion in an otherwise fragmented world. The rock carving surfaces at Nämforsen constitute advertisements *for* and *of* a cosmological system linking together hunter-gatherer groups normally dispersed and perhaps associated with different and much smaller, and iconologically simpler carving and painting sites with restricted meaning content within their individual territories. It forms the only rock carving location in northern Sweden in which the cosmology of the world is laid out in full and in the process of which the different clans using the ritual areas of the rock carvings become integrated and related to each other. The other rock carving sites are not only almost entirely dominated by one de*sign* form, that of the elk, but they also lack any system of motif transformation or fabulous forms. It is significant that at these other carving and painting sites, on which other depictions than elk are virtually lacking, the form of the elk should undergo a much greater degree of elaboration than at Nämforsen, with the production of an X-ray perspective (see the discussion above, p. 89 and Figure 41). These depictions of ribs, hearts, life-lines and sexual organs of the elk emphasize this animal as a potent source of symbolism and classificatory possibilities, acting both as signifier and signified, undoubtedly connected with its economic significance as the life-blood of these societies. Apart from Nämforsen, a metaphoric transformational extension of this symbolism seems to occur only at the Stornorrfors site – significantly the only other site to possess boats. Here elk ribs are emphasized over and over again while the boats, consisting entirely of double-line forms, possess elaborated internal hull division, a symbolic transference and correspondence between the natural and the cultural; the ribs of an elk find their equivalence in the ribs of a boat. In this connection it is interesting to note the lack of internal elk body parts at Nämforsen correlates with a lack of elaborate internal boat hull or rib division. Emphasis is instead placed on the elk head on boat prows, a feature that occurs only once at Stornorrfors.

10

AN ANALYTICS OF POWER

A Marxist hermeneutic – the decipherment by historical materialism of the cultural monuments and traces of the past – must come to terms with the certainty that all the works of class history as they have survived and been transmitted to people the various museums, canons and 'traditions' of our own time, are all in one way or another profoundly ideological, have all had a vested interest in and a functional relationship to social formations based on violence and exploitation; and that, finally, the restoration of the meaning of the greatest cultural monuments cannot be separated from a passionate and partisan assessment of everything that is oppressive in them and that knows complicity with privilege and class domination, sustained with the guilt not merely of culture in particular but of History itself as one long nightmare.

(Jameson 1981: 299)

Linguistic and material culture texts are not just systems of representations whose meanings are to be structurally analysed through a depth hermeneutics and dialogically appropriated. They are also to be objected to, critically analysed and discussed, for texts embody ideologies and powers which form an essential part of their nature. Ideology may be understood as a set of representations relating to politics, a form of signification legitimating social relations of dominance and serving to reproduce these relations. This raises questions of power, domination and the critique of domination largely absent from Gadamer's and Ricoeur's hermeneutics. The sociohistorical world is a field in which 'meaning' may be manipulated in relation to repression. We need to shift over from a dialogic understanding to uncover the relations of force in signifying practices.

149

'ART', POWER, VIOLENCE

For any Marxist criticism of literature or cultural products such as artistic production, the category of the superstructure in a layer-cake base/superstructure model of society has presented serious problems. This is because, if the superstructure is simply to be derived from and reflects the underlying economic base, then there is little place or necessity for a Marxist approach to the non-economic. All that is required is a pigeonholing of cultural products in relation to various modes of production or an assertion of a series of homologies between the economic and the cultural. There is little conceptual space for considering cultural products as representing spheres of significance and meaning on their own, since the sphere of cultural practices in the superstructure (politics, law, religion, art, etc.) is simply held to reflect and further processes of economic domination and determination. Religion is simply an opiate for the masses, the juridical system a means of protecting the interests of those who control the forces of production, etc. The forces and relations of production operate to determine the social totality as a whole which is reflected in the cultural forms produced. The superstructure is in a sense pure ideology – an unreal tissue of appearances projected by an underlying economic reality serving to legitimate and reproduce the economic base. The relationship between economic base and superstructure is one of a simple mechanical causality. Changes in the former are reflected in the latter.

Althusser's work (Althusser and Balibar 1970; Althusser 1977) and the legacy that it has left Marxist literary criticism, anthropology and archaeology is important primarily because it created a fresh intellectual space within Marxist theory to rethink the totality through a framework in which the superstructure was to be granted a relative autonomy, with the economic base conceived as determinant only 'in the last instance'. This framework clearly requires the study of superstructural aspects of the totality in their own right rather than as manifestations of an economic essence. Althusser's conception of the social totality was as a structure in dominance, with notions of dominance and determination clearly separated. While in the capitalist mode of production the economy can be conceived as both dominant and determinant, in pre-capitalist social forms the categories forming the superstructure at any one moment, such as ideology or politics, may be conceived as dominant, with the economic determinant only in the last instance. Clearly, then, the analysis of superstructural relations in these social forms becomes even more significant in understanding the nature of social production and reproduction. The overall problem with the Althusserian framework, particularly thrown into focus in the analysis of pre-capitalist social formations, is that either the ideological and the political are autonomous, thus possessing their own effectivity, in which case we cannot define relations of production as being simply economic, or they are not autonomous and in that case analysis of the social relations of production must always be primary. A notion of 'relative autonomy' cannot be sustained. These and other arguments have led to the dissolution of the Althusserian framework and today there is no single position within Marxist theory that can be regarded as supplanting it. In this sense Marxist theory is in a state of disarray and some would term this a crisis in confidence. What we have today is a plethora of different Marxisms wedded to structuralist, post-structuralist and phenomenological brides. However, in place of the single dogmatic position which everyone could agree on or subscribe to and comfortably label as 'Marxist', a new vitality has been introduced by extending important concepts and elements of Marxist theory in new directions.

This is particularly important in the analysis of pre-capitalist social formations, in which the separation of the economy, politics, ideology, religion has always had to rest on an artificial imposition of categories more suited to nineteenth-century capitalism. It is better to collapse the base/superstructure model altogether and avoid any separation of the economic and the non-economic and material/non-material conditions. We are left with a position of dialectical determination and mediation in which, for example, the economic, the political and the religious inhere in each other and together determine the nature of social life. To derive processes of social reproduction or transformation from a sector labelled 'economic' is a mistake and it is equally misguided to posit a pure determination of the social by cultural or political processes.

'Art' is a western cultural category unfortunately linked to romantic and mystical notions of 'genius', of free 'creative' processes, a practice uniquely different from other sorts of production. Here I regard 'art' as a social production arising from determinate historical and social circumstances and dialectically related to them. It is to be conceived as both an 'economic' and an 'ideological' form. In other words, in pre-capitalist social formations in particular, art is not just a series of representations of the world but may act powerfully to structure and restructure socioeconomic practices in a material way. It is not a separate sphere of activity. Because it may play such a crucial role in the production and reproduction of social relations in small-scale societies, it may also be important in reproducing and sustaining relations of dominance.

Art as a system of representations may be held to perform work in the world. It is not only a material production but has material effects. In Gadamer's and Ricoeur's hermeneutics there is an unhelpful insistence on the category of the individual subject, to whose sensibilities the art work is to be related. This leads to the danger that meaning cannot be adequately conceived as a collective process. What is required instead is, as Jameson argues, a positive hermeneutic based upon a notion of collectivities rather than individual subjects and their personalized experiences (Jameson 1981: 286).

In discussing ideology in art forms it is important to avoid a conception of the receiver who views or 'reads' the work as some inert or passive material on which a manipulatory system operates to produce a 'false consciousness' of the social. Jameson usefully suggests that we understand the power of ideology in terms of a process of 'compensatory exchange', in which the receiver of the art work is offered specific gratifications in return for his or her consent to passivity. The position of those in power and authority need not be accepted as preordained or right but it nevertheless has to be regarded as legitimate in some way. Art works as politically active creations playing a role in maintaining relations of dominance must offer substantial incentives for ideological adherence to a particular position which legitimizes the interests of the few in the name of the many. Ideological forms may characteristically take on a Utopian character, forging a notion of the unity of a collectivity and communal interests that do not exist. A particularly apposite example is given by Barthes (1973) in relation to denotative and significative levels of meaning: there is no 'innocent' or transparent fact or event. All facts and events 'speak' to their culturally conditioned observers and participants. The meaning of processes of signification may in some circumstances be analogous for those who 'produce' and 'consume' cultural sign systems. It is particularly through processes of connotative signification that signs act in a different way, asymmetrically, becoming ideological, linked to the maintenance of power and processes of social domination. This is what Barthes refers to by the term 'myth' or 'depoliticized speech' since in fact reality is always invested with relations of power (politics). He provides a particularly cogent example of the shift from denotation to connotation in discussing a cover of the magazine *Paris-Match*:

> I am at the barber's, and a copy of *Paris-Match* is offered to me. On the cover, a young Negro in a French uniform is saluting, with his eyes uplifted, probably fixed on a fold of the tricolour. All this is the *meaning* of the picture. But, whether naively or not, I see very well what it signifies to me: that France is a great Empire, that all her sons, without any colour discrimination, faithfully serve under her flag, and that there is no better answer to the detractors of an alleged colonialism than the zeal shown by this Negro in serving his so-called oppressors.
>
> (Barthes 1973: 116)

DISCOURSE, MATERIAL CULTURE

I will refer to discourse as something which comes in between *langue* and *parole*: situated speaking and writing or actual language use in which groups or classes of users are differentially related to *langue* and do not participate in it equally. Pêcheux (1982) has underlined the fact that speaking and writing are not only instruments of communication (as in an idealized scenario of sender/ receiver of a message) but also of non-communication. In particular the discourse of linguistic communities is related to power–knowledge–truth strategies and is to be connected to struggles and divisions in society. It is readily apparent that discourse is related to processes of domination and resistance, particularly in class-divided societies such as capitalism. Those who cannot speak the 'right' language, as fostered in educational systems, become subordinate to those who can. Discourse is not only bound up in a general way with divisions of labour but quite specifically with different social institutions and academic 'disciplines'. These create specific sites of communication which establish the place and role of the sender and receiver of messages and determine what kinds of messages may be deemed appropriate and what should be outlawed and banished. Saussure's *langue/parole* distinction is both highly general and abstract, an idealization. Discourse, we might say, is the specific material site in which the relationship between language and speech is actually played out. Theoretical linguistics cannot deal adequately with the realization of language in the world. Discourse analysis, on the other hand, is a manner of approaching language use as a materialist practice embodying power and ideology. Another way of thinking about this is to understand that when we move from the morphology of the sentence and syntax to meaning, we leave behind a *langue* to which ideally everyone bears an equivalent relation, to consider the material site of the enunciation. A sentence is not just a collection of linguistic signs to be understood in their difference. The meaning in it is a predicative act in which something is relayed to someone in the here and now.

The meaning of the sentence takes on an active character according to the wider discursive formation (arena of writing/speaking) in which it is situated, so that the same sentence and the same words can take on different meanings in relation to the social conditions of their enunciation and reception. Meaning is not neutral but relates to institutions, groups and struggles.

Conspicuously absent from the two approaches taken so far has been any mention of repressive power. Nämforsen is being represented as the creation of a structural and symbolic logic which maps human relations in terms of natural species and cultural objects, a process involving the objectification of the social through a visual medium. Alternatively, it has been argued that it forges social and cosmological cohesion through establishing an ontology of resemblances at a central ritual aggregation site. In both cases the structure of the argument has focused on the way in which the rock carvings are used as a means of communication. The positive effects of ambiguity have been stressed – permitting and helping connections through a general system of resemblances. I now want to shift attention to the manner in which the rock carvings *do* something, i.e. have active social and political effects in the world. Basically this amounts to stating that whether or not the rock carvings are 'good to think' they may certainly be regarded as 'good to act'. Nämforsen may be regarded as a discourse *in*, *for* and *of* dominance. The notion of ambiguity may now be understood in another sense: ambiguity as equivocation, as a process halfway to lying.

'Thinking with' and 'acting with' may, of course, be regarded as complementary but not equivalent aspects of objectification. Miller (1987: 40–1, 81–2) makes clear that objectification processes can be conceptualized in two contrasted ways. First, objectification may be regarded as a token of *power to* i.e. an ability to utilize a resource in a manner which creates possibilities of inalienability between persons and things. It is simply a process of externalization, whereby individuals or groups consciously or unconsciously are in a state of 'becoming'. Through their material praxis and cultural representations people project themselves. Objectification is the means by which any expression of activity takes on a material form and it is only through the realization of form (substance), whether in language or material culture, that subjects can conceive of themselves and others. From the accounts given so far, Nämforsen is then a process by which people come to know the world that they have themselves produced through their social praxis. But this presupposes that structure, ritual, symbolism and cosmology have got nothing to do with power over others. A second sense of objectification will be explored in this section, objectification as relating to an exercise of domination and control in which power becomes exercised over others through material praxis. In other words objectification becomes part of a process in which control over specific material forms by particular interest groups furthers the repressive power and dominance of these groups. But these two senses of the use of the term objectification are by no means exclusive and we may speak of a constant dialectic between objectification as externalization and as alienation. Thus Nämforsen structures, orders and provides meaning for the social world of those groups using the site. It can also be regarded as an example of the exercise of symbolic violence. The islands at Nämforsen can be viewed not only as bounded sacred sites but containers of power, the symbolism not simply that of sense and meaning, but as involved in the dynamics of social practices acting dialectically to structure and restructure social relations.

SOCIAL COMPLEXITY, TECHNOLOGICAL SIMPLICITY

In order to understand this process a more fine-grained theoretical conceptualization of the nature of hunter-fisher-gatherer social formations in northern Sweden needs to be introduced. There is no evidence indicating residential stability for longer periods than a season. The picture that seems to arise from the most detailed archaeological study of hunter-gatherer subsistence–settlement systems in northern Sweden is one of a seasonally shifting pattern of

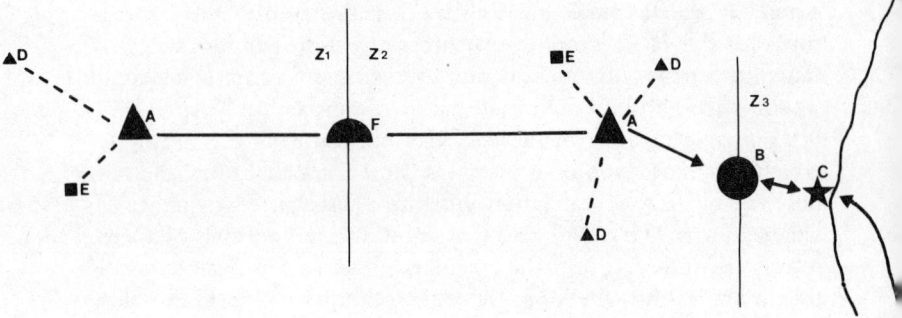

Figure 49 Hypothetical synchronic model of hunter-fisher-gatherer subsistence and settlement systems along river valleys in northern Sweden.
Zone 1 (Z1): Mountain foothill area; zone 2 (Z2): Inland forest area; zone 3
(Z3): Coastal area with pockets of tilled land and farming communities. A:
hunter-gatherer residential camps, seasonally occupied; B: aggregation site
and exchange locale; C: coastal farming settlement; D: hunter-gatherer
exploitation camp; E: hunting station; F: transient camp used along east–
west hunter-gatherer river valley-based settlement shifts. Lines with arrows
indicate exchange linkages between hunter-gatherer and farmer groups and
between the latter and southern Scandinavian communities by boat.
(Diagram partly based on original research by Forsberg 1985: Figure 7.4,
along the Ume and Lule river valleys)

social groups, each associated with and symbolically relating to a
major river system (Forsberg 1985). This is a pattern which is also
historically documented for most Saami groups (e.g. Vorren 1980).
Forsberg has put forward a synchronic model based on detailed
analyses of the material from the Ume and Lule river systems for
the period around 1500 BC and later suggesting spring, summer and
winter settlements in the forest areas and possibly autumn settlement in the mountain foothills, each with major residential camps
and task-specific sites, with a major aggregation site at the terminal
ends of these riverine systems. Such a model would equally well
apply to the Ångerman river system immediately to the south, with
Nämforsen constituting a communal central aggregation site for
territorially dispersed groups (see Figure 49).

Recently conceptions of prehistoric hunter-fisher-gatherer subsistence and settlement systems have been moving further and
further away from traditional approaches invoking a highly mobile

156

and flexible egalitarian band model based on groups such as the !Kung, Mbuti or Hadza, towards a realization that these social forms may well be late developments arising as a response to sustained and long-term interaction with non-hunter-gatherer groups. Bender (1978, 1985, 1989) has consistently stressed the importance of alliance and exchange systems in hunter-gatherer societies, with their inbuilt potential for social elaboration, including the development of definite forms of social inequality both within groups articulated in terms of gender and age and between groups in relation to alliance structures. Alliances and exchange networks are part of the process by which human labour becomes deployed, evaluated and socially appropriated. They not only foster social ties but also create the structural conditions for social dependency: competitive gift giving and feasting create cycles of social debt which require reciprocation. Built into the very nature of group alliance systems is a pattern in which the elders may socially appropriate part of the labour product in return for bride-price or prestige goods and there is always a possibility for local production to intensify in order to meet the requirements of feasting/alliance/ritual/group aggregation cycles. Gender and age divisions within groups provide a basis for the grafting of social power and control and this may be systematically linked with control over ritual information deemed essential to the well-being of the group.

Lévi-Strauss once commented:

> I see no reason why mankind should have waited until recent times to produce minds of the calibre of a Plato or an Einstein. Already over two or three hundred thousand years ago, there were probably men of a similar capacity, who were of course not applying their intelligence to the solution of the same problems as these more recent thinkers, they were probably more interested in kinship!
>
> (Lévi-Strauss 1968: 351)

As this quotation implies it is important to avoid any correlation between technological simplicity, hunter-gatherer economic strategies and a lack of cultural and social elaboration. Even a cursory examination of ethnographies demonstrates that no such correlation between the technological, the economic, the social and the political can be made. Nowhere is this clearer than among Australian Aboriginal groups in which elaborate kinship systems are intimately linked to intricate cosmologies, myth and ritual practices (see pp. 164–7).

EXCHANGE AND ETHNICITY

In Part I the carvings were considered in detail. Their relationship to the contemporary settlement at Nämforsen and to other hunter-gatherer settlements and rock carving sites in northern Sweden was also examined. But this remains insufficient and the question of intersocietal as well as intrasocietal interactions requires investigation within a wider context. Social reproduction and transformation take place as much between as within social totalities, which can be conceived as being linked within a wider system that transcends them. As Rowlands points out (1987), this is not just a question of interrelations between social formations considered as discrete entities; processes of interaction may also be vital to a consideration of the manner in which individual social formations reproduce and constitute themselves over time. Conscious identity and social boundedness may be forged by outside forces. Concomitantly it is impossible to separate out an understanding of the form and nature of social formations from their interaction with other social formations. Processes of production and exchange are intimately linked and may be articulated in terms of a larger system of reproduction both incorporating and transcending local social units.

Christiansson (1961), Baudou (1973), Anderson (1976) and others have proposed that during the Stone Age and the Bronze Age (i.e. during the period in which the rock carvings were produced) there may have been separate coastal and interior economic and social systems in northern Sweden. In the coastal region some agriculture was practised from the middle Neolithic onwards in small pockets of land (Baudou 1982) but in the interior only hunting, fishing and gathering. So we have a contrast between what have been termed 'Neolithic' and 'sub-Neolithic' populations (Baudou 1973: 19). Such a coastal–inland economic distinction continued into the Bronze Age, when the distinction between coast and inland regions becomes clearer. We find large numbers of southern Scandinavian grave forms (large stone cairns) along the coasts but none in the interior. Nämforsen, situated at the end of a long narrow inlet of the sea, can be considered to have a somewhat ambivalent status – both coastal and interior – and perhaps this unusual position accounts, at least in part, for the choice of this location.

From the middle Neolithic onwards, and very broadly correlated with the establishment of pockets of farming activity, an exchange system of some kind existed between coastal areas of northern Sweden and southern Scandinavia. In view of the enormous distances

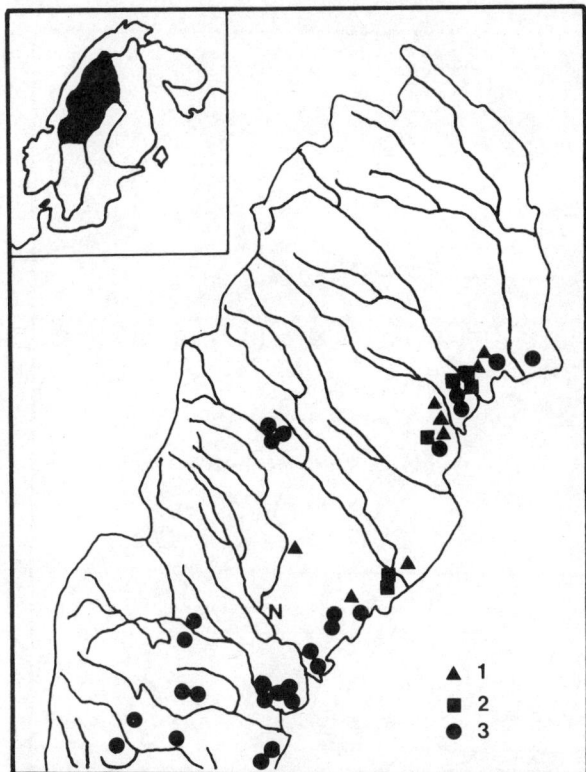

Figure 50 The distribution of southern Scandinavian imported artefacts in northern Sweden. 1: stone battle-axes; 2: flint finds; 3: double-edged axes (Information from Christiansson 1961: Figure 15)

involved and the dense forest cover, this must have been maritime exchange. Significant numbers (over 350) of flint axes and chisels have been discovered, largely along the coast, but some in the interior (Figure 50). As flint does not occur naturally in northern Sweden it must have been introduced from elsewhere, the most probable source being southern Scandinavia (Clark 1948, 1952: 252–6; Christiansson 1961; Christiansson and Broadbent 1975), and a very few daggers and arrowheads of possibly Russian flint have also been identified (Huggert 1984). The majority of the axes are found in ritual hoards, unused and in many cases unpolished. Some may have been broken up for subsequent use as scrapers or other tools. With regard to the directionality of the exchange, some

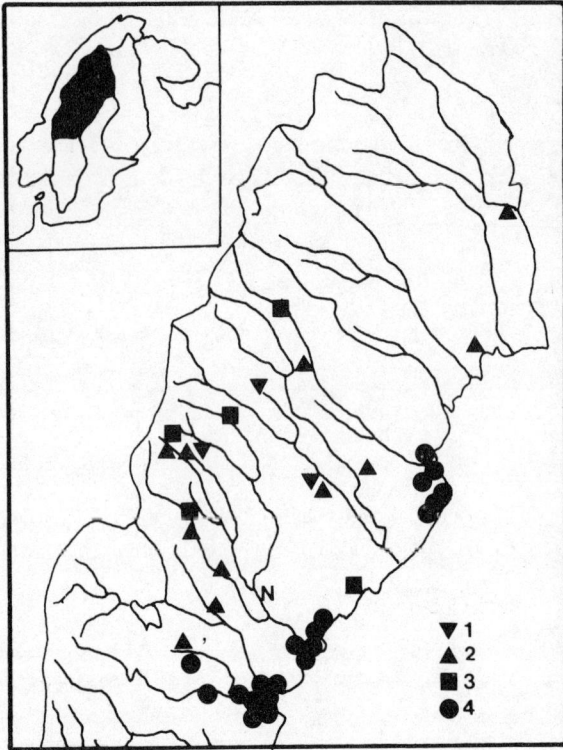

Figure 51 The distribution of bronzes and bronze moulds in northern Scandinavia. 1: arctic mould for celt; 2: celt; 3: mould for dagger blade or spear head; 4: metal find (Information from Kristiansen 1987: Figure 8.6)

objects of red Ångerman slate have been discovered as far south as Blekinge, southern Sweden. We know that copper and tin did not occur in an exploitable form in Scandinavia and that all this metal, ultimately derived from sources in central and western Europe, must have been imported by boat to southern Sweden. In this respect it is pertinent to note with Moberg (1965) that the only carving sites in northern Scandinavia where boats are depicted are near or on the coasts. There are no boats at inland sites.

The vast majority of bronze finds are from southern Scandinavia; only very small numbers of bronzes are known from northern Sweden (Figure 51). The northern Swedish bronzes can be divided into two types – those with an origin in farming societies in central or eastern Russia and those from south Scandinavia. The southern Scandinavian bronzes are clustered exclusively along the Bothnian coast while those of 'Arctic type' or of Russian origin are found in the interior.

I have already noted (see p. 51) Malmer's comments about exchange in relation to Nämforsen and southern Scandinavia and that the most likely exchange items would have been furs and elk hides. Olaus Magnus in his *Historia* (1554) mentions thousands of elk hides being sent from northern Scandinavia across the sea (Hallström 1960: 376). Furs are also the most likely items exchanged to the east for the Arctic bronzes.

Kristiansen (1987) has recently reviewed the evidence from Scandinavia in terms of centre–periphery relations coupled with the gradual development of a prestige goods exchange system. To what extent the terms centre and periphery can be adequately used to describe relations between northern and southern Sweden during the time period under consideration remains problematic. There may very well be a real danger here in extrapolating from anachronistic historically derived models. The modern concept of centre–periphery is far better suited to describe the situation in Scandinavia after the period of state formation in the south – a much later development. It seems preferable to focus on exchange, interaction and the formation of ethnic identities in the Bronze Age of Scandinavia without introducing a series of inappropriate concepts. To view the hunter-gatherer communities of northern Scandinavia as in any sense peripheral to the Bronze Age communities in the south does little to aid our understanding of the processes involved.

Very limited numbers of southern Scandinavian or Russian metal items have been found in northern Scandinavia (less than fifty items in northern Sweden – Christiansson 1961: 132). This is unlikely to be entirely attributable to sampling problems. More bronzes are likely to be discovered in the south because of its much denser population, more widespread agriculture, road building, housing developments, etc. However, the enormous disparity in quantities of bronze finds cannot be entirely attributable to this. It is more probable that a series of unequal and exploitative exchange relations existed between the northern hunter-gatherer communities and the farming communities with whom they were involved to both the south and the east.

Olsen (1984: 215–17, 1985: 28–9) has suggested that the formation of distinct ethnic identities over large areas was an important process in northern Scandinavia during the early Bronze Age and he again draws a primary contrast between inland and coastal groups. Synchronous with the appearance of Arctic bronzes in the north, a relatively homogeneous 'asbestos ceramic' tradition became established. This ceramic tradition, like the Arctic bronzes, was absent from the Bothnian coast. The postulate is that material items – the bronzes and the ceramics – were being actively utilized to mark out ethnic difference and forge links with the metal-producing farmers in the east. Consequently the situation is not only that of an economic divide between the Bothnian coastal farmers and the inland hunter-gatherers but one that is being reinforced symbolically through material forms and the directionalities of exchange items.

In a world where, compared with today, material objects were generally few, transient (axes break, harpoons splinter, pots fragment) and relatively unelaborated, cultural forms of such material permanence, complexity and obvious antiquity as the rock carvings would have had immense significance in linking together present, past and future. The rock carvings at Nämforsen are quite obviously immovable and the site must have been used again and again. Part of this use seems to have involved constant reference to the past. The repetition of the same de*sign* forms may suggest that change is being disguised as timelessness. Amongst these dispersed and what must have been relatively mobile hunter-fisher-gatherer populations the visual images in the carvings provided pooled ritual information considered essential to the continued existence of the social order, a 'hoarding' of information. Following Root (1983), Hood (1988) has underlined the connection between stationary information, to which potential consumers must come, and the development of relations of dominance. Knowledge that is restricted in space is not accessible to all:

> Through the creation of stationary information sources ... material culture articulates with social relations to *construct* social and ideological space while it is simultaneously *constrained* by that space. ... Inevitably, there are incongruities between knowledge and space; these incongruities in access to knowledge are fundamental to power relations and the ongoing structuration of social relations.
>
> (Hood 1988:68–9)

In this respect we can regard Nämforsen as spatially restricted information that is fixed and cannot be exchanged. To sketch a possible scenario for relations between different social groups: the inland hunter-fisher-gatherers may have been gradually sucked and incorporated into a much wider exchange system over which they had very little control and to which they had to accommodate themselves. This may have involved exchange with coastal communities, in turn involved in an exchange relation with elite groups in southern Scandinavia (Figure 49) as well as indirectly with farmers to the east. Originally Nämforsen may have started as a fairly small rock carving site utilized by only one or a few groups. Contact with groups using other carving sites situated on other river systems, such as the Stornorrfors site on the Ume river to the north, is perhaps indicated by the occurrence of elks with internal body divisions on the central Brådön carving surface (Figure 19). Later the site, already in use as a summer salmon fishing location and ritual carving area, took on an additional role as a major regional aggregation centre, in which elk hides and furs (collected during the previous hunting season – hence the absence of elk bones at the Nämforsen settlement site itself) were exchanged for prestige goods such as bronzes, flint, and no doubt other items leaving now no trace in the archaeological record.

These prestige goods were too few in quantity to be of any economic significance whatsoever or to provide a basis for stimulating the development of any substantial degree of political hierarchization between local hunter-fisher-gatherer groups. Their primary importance would have been as circulating symbolic tokens conferring prestige in competitive gift giving, marriage exchanges and feasting cycles. Virtually all of this exotic material from the south evidently remained in coastal areas while only items from the east seem to have been utilized by inland groups in any appreciable quantities. However, the important point is that the inland hunter-fisher-gatherers found themselves for the first time drawn into continued and sustained contact with coastal agricultural populations and perhaps even with individuals from southern Scandinavia engaged in maritime exchange.

With the incorporation of the inland hunter-fisher-gatherers within an exchange system linking northern and southern Sweden and the hunter-fisher-gatherers and coastal farmers, the inland groups became inevitably exposed to alien populations. These contacts may have been metaphorically represented by a different symbol set, including boats, shoe soles and scythe-like tools. Contact with very different populations had major consequences.

163

Symbolically it required the incorporation within the already existing symbol set of elks, fish, birds, and stick-line human bodies at Nämforsen of a fresh set of motifs to make cosmological sense of the new contacts within pre-existing mythologies. An alien symbol (the circle–cross) was inserted on the central carving surface at Brådön and a triangular human body to symbolize the outsiders on the same rock surface. The relationship between insiders and outsiders, land and sea people, was primarily signified by the form of the boat but also in distinctions between the stick-line and the triangular human bodies. Significantly, the outsiders are portrayed in the liminal spaces of the rock carving surfaces as novices – hence the lack of phallic representations on the 'triangular' bodies. This in itself implies that a hierarchy of between-group social relations was perceived by the indigenous group. The fresh de*signs* were linked with the existing cosmological system by the portrayal of elk heads on boats, and by definite associations between elks and boats made in a variety of ways, as already outlined. Not only did the hunter-fisher-gatherers at Nämforsen accommodate their economic system to the demands of an exchange system for which they received very little in return, but they even restructured their cosmological and symbolic system.

The incorporation of a fresh symbol set within those already existing gave those individuals and/or groups responsible for producing the new carvings an increased basis for social dominance and control through the exploitation of spatial inequalities in access to the ritual knowledge embodied in the carvings, reinforcing their social status *vis-à-vis* other local hunting and gathering groups. This developing status elevation provided compensation for basic inequalities in exchange relations with the coastal populations and/or southern Scandinavian traders. The carving surfaces were thus actively used through time to foster strategies of social control requiring the manipulation, structuring and restructuring of the de*signs*.

AUSTRALIA: ANCESTORS, KNOWLEDGE, POWER

The Australian example provides one of the few instances we have to hand of contemporary hunter-gatherer groups who also produce rock art. An exploration of the relationship between Aboriginal social structures, ritual practices and artistic production has general relevance as a further source of insight into the types of relationship that are being considered here. Among Aboriginal groups there exists an enormous disparity between an elaborated kin and ideological apparatus and a relatively simple economic structure. An extremely complex totemic geography maps people and groups into the landscape (Strehlow 1970; Berndt 1976). Ancestral beings, who are conceived as combining human and animal attributes or are capable of transforming themselves from animal to human form and vice versa and from animate to inanimate objects such as rocks, often move for vast distances through the Australian desert. Each group has responsibility for carrying out ceremonies at particular sites visited by or associated with these ancestral beings. Several groups may share the same track and often what distinguishes groups is the collection of tracks that run through their territories. Each group has a unique combination of totems, each of which individually may be shared with other groups (Layton 1981: 87). Nature is transposed into a pattern imbued with symbolism and meaning and connected with ancestral beings. Murphy has noted that

> Art mediates between the ancestral past, or Dreaming, when the form of the land was created by the actions of mythical Ancestral Beings, and the present. Art is an extension of the Ancestral Past into the present and is one of the main ways in which ideas or information about the Ancestral Past is transmitted from one human generation to the next.
>
> (Murphy 1989: 144)

The important point about this is that the ancestral past cannot be directly experienced. It can only be known through the representations made of it. This past is both part of the present and yet cut off from it. The present becomes legitimized and naturalized through reference to the past. Each descent group possesses a set of sacred sites imbued with the spiritual power of the ancestors and controls access to these sites. Aboriginal rock art sites themselves become embedded in a whole set of values and rituals associated with the wider totemic landscape (Stanner 1965). The land is not conceived as belonging to people; rather, the people belong to a marriage section, which in turn belongs to a supernatural reality represented by totems and sacred sites. The landscape is symbolically constructed from the relationship of different totemic groups to it. What is stable here is not the relationship of people within groups that may change but the relationship between groups.

Aboriginal art and its meaning were socially controlled and knowledge about the full significance of this art remained an exclusive religious property controlled by older men and displayed in ritual practices. Senior men regularly visit sites to ensure their protection and perform rituals (Layton 1989: 2). The power of older men was derived from their ability to control meaning and direct ritual practices:

> The most central acts of creative autonomy and potency occur within the male cult where the individual constructs or renews ancestral objects .... . Through these operations, in which he becomes 'ancestor-like', he can contribute in certain cere- monies to the reconstitution, or life-maintenance of the people, flora and fauna of the countryside.

> (Munn 1970: 159)

In many groups such as the Walbiri of the central Australian desert women do produce art but there is a significant contrast between the forms and nature of representations executed by women and those carried out by men, almost always in the absence of women. Women's representations often take the form of sand stories: patterns drawn in the sand on camp sites telling about day-to-day activities or generalized activities of the ancestors. Men's represen- tations are predominantly concerned with the tracking of specific ancestors across the landscape, by reference to which the territorial claims of the groups are established and projected back into the past. It is only through secret male rituals that the identity of key ancestors is learnt. There are two planes involved here, of differing significance. One (the woman's) is particularistic and personal, the other (the men's) is cosmic and societal with its locus in patrilineal descent groups (Munn 1973: 27). Once initiated, males are able to take an active part in identifying and maintaining group-orientated ancestral identities and their relation to land. Women cannot do this and their interests are 'guarded' by the men. *Guruwari* is both the name for graphic designs representing the ancestors (these designs are primarily owned by men) and a term referring to ancestors, fertility power, the power of generation: an abstract property left by the ancestors as they journeyed across the territory. A direct link is thus made between visible representational forms controlled by men and invisible potent powers essential to social reproduction left by the ancestors which can only be mediated by men. A pregnant woman is said to have been entered by the *guruwari* of a particular ancestor (Munn 1973: 29, 214ff.) and in this manner even the sexual reproductive powers of women are controlled and appropriated by men.

Power in Aboriginal society was and is structured ritually in relation to ceremonies, myth, song and art. Women are excluded from access to control of ritual property and their distribution through marriage sections is controlled by older men. Bern (1979) argues for a double system of dominance of women by men and of juniors by elders in which 'women only collect what men's religious practice has made available' (Bern 1979: 125). Art becomes politically manipulated through its seclusion from women in ritual practices and the gradual revelation of the knowledge contained in it to novices establishing links between paintings, sites, myths and ancestral beings (Munn 1973; Layton 1985, 1989). Older males articulate power through the two institutions to which restricted access is socially and politically most effective: religious ceremonies and the right to bestow wives. Just as junior men are denied wives, they are denied access to the esoteric knowledge contained in ritual ceremonies and the art.

DOMINATION AND THE BODY

One aspect of the relation of the visual structure of the carvings to structures of social reproduction, already explored above, was the ideological reinforcement of patterns of social dominance and control between hunter-fisher-gatherer groups using the site. As a central ritual aggregation site, however, we can also envisage it operating in terms of power relations within groups playing upon gender and age distinctions.

Gender and sex need to be carefully distinguished. The latter can be regarded as a physiological difference between male and female which cannot be altered. The former refers to a set of learned action patterns. Gender, then, is distinct from sex – a culturally and symbolically constituted category distinction always invested with the power of meaning, meaning that may be naturalized and legitimized through ideology and ritual. Among gatherer-hunter groups Collier and Rosaldo (1981) have argued there is an explicit disjunction between a male world on the one hand and a hetero-sexual world on the other while Ortner and Whitehead stress that economic and kinship-marriage relations ramify upon sex gender ideology as these relations are filtered through the perspective of the male ego situated within the prestige structure (or structures) of the society under consideration.

(Ortner and Whitehead 1981: 19–20)

In relation to the above discussion it is of importance to note that gender distinctions are both marked and pervasive in all historically documented northern Eurasian hunter-gatherer groups and pastoralist groups and that this is invariably linked with an image of women as ritually impure and polluting, contaminating the male hunter and his prey. A notion of female impurity is accompanied by an extensive series of taboos and restrictions. To mention a few examples of these practices: among Siberian Tungus groups a woman can be held to be the cause of a lack of success in hunting if she happens to be near the prey or if her odour lingers on the hunter's equipment. The Lamuts of Verkhoyansk did not even permit the husband of a pregnant woman to go near killed wild deer (Tugolukov 1978: 424–5; see also Jochelson 1926). Nganasan and Enets groups prohibited women from looking into the eyes of wild deer for fear they would give birth to non-human monsters (Simčenko 1978: 507). Among the Saami of northern Sweden, Finland and Norway women were similarly regarded as ritually unclean and this legitimated numerous sanctions on their behaviour. Blood was at the heart of sanctions and because of women's ritual impurity, rationalized through reference to polluting menstrual blood, they could not approach the sacred places where sacrifices were performed; they could not fish in lakes considered sacred; they should not cross the path of a hunter; they should not cross the path where the sacred shaman's drum (*runebommen*) had been carried or the path of a man going to or arriving from a sacrifice. They should not approach the *påssio/boassju*, the holy place in the tent, or use the back entrance reserved for the hunter who brought both the prey and his hunting gear through this entrance. The exclusion of the women from the prey sometimes even resulted in males cooking the meat. The ritually important bear-hunt ceremony involving searching, killing, slaughtering, cooking, eating and finally burying the bear further underlined male ritual dominance. The bear was cooked and prepared in a special tent from which women were excluded. Only males could eat the front quarters of the bear and for one year no woman could use the reindeer which had pulled the bear to the tent. The hunter who had killed the bear could not have sexual intercourse with his wife for three days afterwards (Rheen 1897: 19, 35–9; Drake 1918; von Düben 1977: 277–84; Vorren and Manker 1979: 160–1; Fjellström 1985; Yates 1989).

Saami ritual knowledge and practices provide simply one example among dozens documented ethnographically of the manner in which relations of domination between men and women ground themselves in conceptions of the body and its substances. Godelier emphasizes that for such relations of domination to be effective those who are dominated must in some way acknowledge their legitimacy: 'a Baruya woman has merely to see the blood start to flow between her thighs for her to hold her tongue and consent to whatever economic, political, and psychological oppression she may be subjected' (Godelier 1986: 233). Sexuality is used simply as a 'ventriloquist's dummy' that can automatically talk about everything and anything and legitimate the social order. Menstrual blood is the irrefutable 'proof' of the impurity of women, who are entirely responsible therefore for their own subordinate status.

The problem with interpreting Nämforsen is that we have a series of depictions which we can sex physiologically as male and a series of unsexed bodies. If we were to assume that in this instance the depiction of sex does bear some relationship to gender roles then the absence of women and settlement scenes at Nämforsen may become explicable from the general perspective sketched above and the direct historical ethnographic evidence. I have already noted that only two figures with a swelling in the belly region may indicate the presence of (pregnant – in which case it is their biological reproductive capacity that is being emphasized) women. The other figures are either phallic or neuter and it would be dangerous to conclude that the absence of a phallus is simply a negative female signifier. The carvings, lacking any indication of settlements, tents, household interiors, etc., are not about the domestic heterosexual world but the cosmological world that appears to be represented as a male preserve. What may be indicated is not simply an arena for male ritual activity but a male cult represented as being for the good of the collectivity.

It seems very likely that the carved islands in the river and the carvings on the northern river banks at Nämforsen would have been used in initiation ceremonies for novices – places of liminal seclusion where vital ritual information was conveyed through instruction and inspection of the cosmologies and mythic stories inscribed on the carved rock surfaces, no doubt involving the ancestors (mythic double-headed elks, elk–humans? etc.). Such information would be controlled by whoever could inspect, produce, or add to the ritual carvings and the meanings and knowledges embedded in them: a secret knowledge to which access was both unequal and dangerous. Secret and hidden knowledge (the carvings out in the violent rapids) may, as Barth (1975) emphasizes, be a potent force in maintaining patterns of social dominance. It is not the content of the knowledge that gives it value so much as the fact that it is not available to all. At Nämforsen the social power of the carvings can also be envisaged as not only being drawn from their evident cosmological content and seclusion but also from the natural power of the location of the site itself, the force of the violent rapids. The natural world reinforces the social world and vice versa. In the spatial ordering of the carved rock surfaces, the order of the social world was both recreated and visually reinforced.

This world seems to be intimately bound up with the forging of solidarity between elder males (perhaps the human stick-line figures with phalluses) and initiates who are in the process of a symbolic transition between states (hence the absence of a phallus on many of the stick-line figures). The carvings embodied ritual knowledge unveiled to initiates, intimately linked to the sexual politics of power and their social reproduction. In the art it is the relationship between men and animals that is being emphasized, men as creators perhaps ritually ensuring the continuing reproduction of the social and natural orders and the intimate relationship between humanity and elks, birds and fish: the most important, highly prized and cosmologically significant animal species. Men are presented as being symbolically closer to the spiritual powers controlling the cosmic order and women are being excluded. The seclusion of the rock carving site away from the settlement and its emphasis on male gender ideology can be regarded as part of a process in which women are distinguished from men both conceptually and in ritual practice. The symbol sets at Nämforsen and their link to power can thus be envisaged as a structured practice, both communicative and constitutive in intent, the consistency of the articulation of the *designs* and their transformational qualities serving to underline appropriate messages about the cosmological world, the ideological naturalization of the place of men and women in the social world, and the link between the sacred and the profane. At Nämforsen we see the legitimation and valorization of male–female divisions of labour through a mythico-religious system dominated by male values and associations, a system in which the age–gender continuum is being cut up into discrete segments. The carvings, through their very durability, constitute a closed universe, an objectification of power, a construction of a durable symbolic capital, a cultural resource naturalizing the present in terms of the past in a space and time divorced from the mundane sphere of everyday activity, constituting a symbolic violence in a situation in which overt violence is impossible.

The reader may have noticed a number of problems with this account. While questions of power and ideology, ethnicity and exchange, domination and the body, have been addressed it quite obviously failed to deal adequately with the *specificity* of the carving surfaces and the relationality of the *design* structures, which the two previous approaches to mediating the text did try to deal with in some detail. The carvings, in effect, become simply subsumed in a much wider account moving away from an in-depth focus on the site of Nämforsen. A distinction was drawn between gender and sex only to be surreptitiously denied and collapsed when an account came to be given of the human bodies. This is obviously inadequate but it does serve to highlight a very real problem of exactly how we are to talk about gender on the sole basis of the carvings themselves with the lack of any other information apart from that provided in ethnohistorical accounts. The sole basis for the claim that a distinction was being created between a heterosexual profane world and a male sacred world associated with the carvings, and excluding women, was the absence of the portrayal of figures that on sexual or by means of other characteristics might be classified as female. Why was this the case? Can it simply be concluded that this signifies the exclusion of women? Might the 'triangular' figures be representing women? The claim that they and the non-phallic stick-line figures represent male initiates is, perhaps, rather too thin. How much weight should be given to ethnohistorical evidence with regard to the domination of women in northern Eurasia, and men's control of the sacred domain? Is this, and the account given, just another example of androcentric bias in reporting and interpretation? Given the dominance of unsexed bodies another answer might be that sex or gender were not significant as regards the portrayal of the human body. Why, then, the phallic representations?

11

CONCLUSIONS

– I cannot accept that you should have completed your discourse with such an open-ended array of possibilities. You have evaded your responsibility to tell us what the carvings do in fact mean. Having told us about structure, cosmological meaning and power, why can't you link all these different facets together to provide a coherent solution that doesn't systematically contradict itself? You are setting up artificial boxes between structure, meaning, power and ideology.

– I could of course do that but why do you not want to be involved in the process? Must you always have everything handed to you on a plate? The 'final' solution? The point that I am really trying to make is that these rock carvings invite a response from us, the infusion of our subjectivity. The carvings present a vocabulary, a cosmological thematics, which not only allows but necessitates a variety of readings. There is no fixed meaning and we must remember that images cannot in fact be reduced to words, 'read'. This 'reading' always results, is intimately linked, with textual production which both inevitably goes beyond the carvings them-selves and yet simultaneously portrays a lack, a failure. I do not present a proper conclusion because it is an impossibility. Under-standing of this material, any 'data' in the human sciences does not conclude. It just stops when we get bored or do not have anything else to say. So I did not set up the different perspectives just for the sake of novelty but to establish a rhetorical point.

– That does not satisfy me at all. I can think of much faster ways of establishing a point of rhetoric. It seems to me that you systemati-cally deny any possibility of truth or certainty in the knowledge relation. This hopeless relativism can only destroy a productive relationship between the past and the present. I want to know what Nämforsen meant, not have a (presumably infinite) number of possibilities thrown at me. Having waded through the previous textual contortions and manipulations of material, that are not even claimed as objective facts by you, a much simpler conclusion can be suggested, a thesis capable of encompassing the entire material in a possibly more satisfactory manner. To me it now seems quite obvious that Nämforsen is yet another tedious example of prehistoric graffiti. Can we not in fact accept that we only have designs (no de*signs*) that were more or less produced at random? To think there might be any deeper meaning to discover is really rather silly. Another scenario automatically suggests itself. On a hot summer's day, while taking a break from salmon fishing, a few hours could simply be whiled away by chipping out the odd elk or two. Sometimes, admittedly, this could be a bit boring and then why not a boat or even the occasional shoe sole? Of course, I'm a sceptic and although I might not actually believe the statement I have just made why shouldn't I make it? Will you incorporate that as just another potential explanation? Do you not in fact end up doing precisely the same thing as you criticized Hallström for – not concluding at all? After an immense textual detour you leave us in the same position as him.

– I believe that any attempt to establish a totalizing framework, accommodating as many observations as possible with, ideally, nothing left out, is doomed to failure. There is always a surplus of meaning. Admittedly the three methodological approaches I have adopted to come to an understanding of the de*signs* (I'll retain that term) may be artificially boxed in. They could be linked in various ways to create perhaps a more embracing solution. But it would still fail to capture everything at Nämforsen and then I would be reduced to the tactic of claiming that what I had dealt with was the most 'essential' or 'important' aspects of the carvings and what I had inevitably left out of the account (to smooth over contradictions) was of no real importance. A totalitarian solution to meaning and understanding is not adequate. All knowledge is socially negotiated, both in the past and the present. Do you really think there is one single meaning to this carving site in prehistory that I have to attempt to mimic or capture in my discourse? I think we can all agree that there is no one meaning to the present, to any cultural

173

artefact (a car or a house). Why should you expect there to be one meaning in the past? Archaeology (or any other human science) is not about certainty. If you expect certainty you are in the wrong boat or stalking the wrong elk! We can only be certain about the banal. I am prepared to accept certainty in the determination of, say, tin content in a bronze, or the determination of species of animals from their bones, but beyond this simple level the term becomes quite irrelevant.

I think that I have established that there is nothing random about the rock carvings and therefore reject your putative fourth conclusion. I have in fact concluded, produced a whole array of different and not necessarily totally contradictory perspectives. I have reinscribed the carvings in fresh discourses, produced a fresh set of meanings. To suggest that I leave you in the same position as Hallström is a complete travesty of everything that I have attempted to do. The carvings are laden with meaning and this meaning is relational, but to establish this relationality we must be prepared to go beyond the surfaces of the individual carvings so we cannot be empirically tied down by them. This was the point of my critique of Hallström – his desire for certainty, for a purely empirically grounded knowledge, led him to silence.

– To be sure you are not being silent; the text that you have produced is a flood of words. Is it anything more than that in fact? At least Hallström left us with some solid data on which your text is entirely dependent. It is this that will stand the test of time long after everyone has forgotten about your own *little* text. Besides, what kind of knowledge relation are you proposing between yourself and the public who might perhaps (unlikely, I suppose) read your book? They will want to be told the meaning of Nämforsen, and by putting forward these different perspectives you are undermining the authority of archaeology as a discipline. Ultimately, when the chips are down, why should they pay you to produce texts such as this? You sap and undermine public confidence in the discipline. At various points you tell us that you will 'put all this into a narrative' and proceed to do so: you're just telling stories, and not particularly exciting ones at that.

– No archaeological text is anything more or less than a flood of words so the question becomes which ones are deemed desirable as metaphoric transformations of the material reality being studied.

You seem to think telling stories is not my proper purpose but I regard any attempt to understand the past as fundamentally involving narrative. Narrative is not an option, rather it has an ontological status: we all live narratives. They are part of life and are represented covertly in virtually all archaeological writing. On a daily basis we create narratives – ordered visions of our lives, past, present and future, with differing and blurred degrees of reality and fantasy. And narrative does not necessarily imply a linear sequence. It rather means putting things in order. Sartre once said somewhere that all ordering is fictive and I think he is essentially correct. Fictions are our way of dealing with the chaos of the brute facts of reality and our life experiences. We construct ordered narrative worlds to understand ourselves and others, emplot experience. We have to tell stories to escape, remake, or find the past or the future. What I've written is not a mirror of the past, nor is it the past as I would wish it to be, but rather a continuation of the (narrative) ordering already found in the carvings I have been investigating. Narrative doesn't involve lies but rather a true representation of the way anyone makes sense of the past. To go back to another point you made, I want to propose that it is men such as Hallström who in fact do what you accuse me of: undermining archaeology's importance. Who could possibly be interested in a sterile catalogue? If this is all archaeology is capable of producing, then public funds should certainly be cut off immediately. I used Hallström as an example. I acknowledge that he produced a tremendous work. The theoretical frameworks that I have been using were hardly available to him when he was producing his text. Of course, he was a man of his time as I am of mine. The problem is that archaeology today is still full of people like Hallström. We have a responsibility to make sense of the past and that does not mean producing just one account and I don't believe this is what people want anyway. No doubt in a flawed manner, what I have nevertheless been attempting in this text is to establish a new relation with the reader – to involve him or her as a producer of the meaning rather than as a consumer. You can take what I have presented and construct your own meaning of and for Nämforsen. This is to assert a more, let us say, democratic relationship between the writer and the reader, the archaeologist and the public. It is to underline the fact that texts, knowledge and power are intimately linked together. No power means no knowledge and no text. The 'authority' of archaeology means precisely that: a will to control, to dominate, set up barriers, disqualify,

alienate. Knowledge is not a property – I cannot describe to you
what it means to know, apart from its being obviously linked to a
certain degree of self-confidence – knowledge is a relation, a social
relation between persons and between persons and things.

– You are contradicting yourself again. Would not the most
democratic relationship between you and the public be to present
them with a book about Nämforsen that was completely blank? As
it is, your text is hardly open – you devote a large section to
criticizing Hallström and, as is usual for you, cannot resist dealing
another blow directed towards functionalist and typologically
orientated archaeologies.

– You are right that my text was not infinitely open. The
'openness' resides in a field of relations. I deliberately created an
entire series of closures to prevent people from adopting positions I
don't like. In writing I must involve myself – it is a form of
objectification of my subjectivity. In involving myself I include my
values and my politics and ultimately this is what this text, our
relation to the past, is all about: what kind of past do we want and
why? I believe it is necessary to fight for and against different pasts
so it is irresponsible to produce a free-floating text or blank text and
endlessly play around with meaning. Nevertheless, I still insist this
does not necessarily imply just one conclusion.

– You have just proposed an unacceptable reductionism. The past,
our relation to it, is much more than present-day values. I admit
these are involved but they ought to be screened out of the analysis
as much as possible. There is a real objective past and our basis for
judgements have to be based on that.

– I agree there is a real past. Nämforsen is there – concrete,
objective substance, also being eroded away. The place, by the way,
is now completely destroyed by the construction of an enormous
power plant, the river most of the year is dry and resembles a
building site, only a few of the carvings are painted in, some
inaccurately – the rest scarcely visible. In case you are interested, it
is scarcely worth visiting today and an immense disappointment.
But to return to your point, our standards of judgement do depend
on the materials of the past but these in no way decide of themselves
the nature of our discourse. All the statements that I have made I

have attempted to relate to the empirical materials, the objective substance of the rock carvings. But these at the same time do not simply stand apart from discourse but are dialectically linked to it. Once I start to write, the meaning of these carvings becomes internal to discourse from the very beginning to the very end. This is why I insisted in the tables and elsewhere on terming the topographical areas of the site carving pages, to remind you constantly this was a text, that there is a gap between the words we use and the things we describe. Naturally the islands etc. are not pages at all and the text at Nämforsen is far from being a linear sequence. I have pointed out that chronometric time and Euclidean space may be quite irrelevant here. These rock carvings do not constitute themselves in any way whatsoever, but I do, and meanings involve values. You cannot bear to hear any more. We had better end this conversation. I would now like to ask you just two questions: What are the limits of discourse, of reasonable speech, and why do you propose that I have transcended them? What is it that you wish to protect, to cherish and hold dear other than a personal image of yourself as a disinterested god who needs to make no choices and possesses no feelings?

Figure 52 Progress and civilization: the power plant and the dead rapids at Nämforsen taken from Notön looking west, August 1988 (Photo: Michael Shanks)

APPENDIX REVIEW:
MATERIAL CULTURE IN A
TEXT

He feels a need for a justification of what he has now managed to produce. The title of his book, its textual form and structure, and mode of analysis are a little complicated and involuted. In this appendix he wants to try and explain why. In the book he attempted to: (i) present a new interpretation of a set of archaeological materials. This is the most conventional aim; (ii) produce a work of theoretical practice; (iii) explore the use of a textual analogy in material culture studies; (iv) experiment in writing the past in a different way; (v) produce a reflexive discourse that turns in on itself. These five aims are very much conjoined and cannot be meaningfully separated out into different moments but to provide a general background he will briefly consider each in turn.

Subtitle: 'The art of ambiguity': he presents a detailed study of the prehistoric rock carvings from one of the most dramatic and largest known sites in Europe: Nämforsen in northern Sweden. He emphasizes the ambiguous (equivocal, enigmatic, cryptic) nature of these carvings which, rather than being considered a failure of understanding, of contemporary interpretative practices, is argued to be constitutive of their meaning, involving a tergiversation or a shifting of senses through different registers and a *double entendre* in which polysemic meaning is created to establish relationships, make connections and establish significances. The ambiguity inherent in the rock carvings cannot be reduced or ignored; it both demands and permits differing sets of interpretations.

The book is a work of materialist theoretical practice. The strategy he adopts is materialist in four fundamental senses. It involves:

(i) an understanding of the materiality of the social world as a lived set of practices;
(ii) a focus on the material inscription of this world as a process of transformative objectification;
(iii) a recognition of the materiality of writing as a textual practice attempting to cope with the world;
(iv) the materiality of the process of interpretation involving the desires of the body and the constraints of the disciplines and institutions to which writing is directed.

179

He wants to try and avoid a split between subject and object, theory and data. He does not want therefore to present an introductory theoretical position in the first part of the book and then proceed to 'apply' it to the rock carvings in the remainder of the text. He tries to stress throughout the exposition that theory is practice, that the materials on which he works are in a perpetual state of becoming through their specific mode of theoretical appropriation. Conceptual outlines of differing interpretative positions are given at a number of points in the text, some with examples drawn from other studies, and then worked through in relation to the rock carvings. In this process of 'working through' a specific medium the positions themselves become both clarified and take on a somewhat different significance. The relation between theory and data is one that remains internal to the research process itself. Both form part of each other in a dialectical *material* relation, while at the same time not collapsing into a unitary form. The data in his study are all *theoretical objects* always already conceptually appropriated and at the same time resisting the frameworks which inevitably attempt to envelop and incorporate them. Any empiricist 'external' test of the validity of the arguments put forward, itself dependent on an idealist conception in which a split between theory and data is presupposed, is therefore quite misguided. Consequently any criticisms of his study which purport to be concerned with 'facts' alone are of absolutely no interest.

In the book he attempts to explore systematically the notion that material culture can be looked at in terms of a textual analogy, as a discourse that is always already written, which the investigator reads and then subsequently rewrites and translates to produce his or her text. In carrying out this project he intends it to be a prolegomenon to future work that will transcend the position presented. The title of the book: 'material culture *and* text' itself indicates this and some of the discussions within it. He is primarily concerned with the relationship between material culture and text and this is to make a rather different case than to make the much stronger claim that material culture is, in fact, a text or can be simply reduced to a series of characteristics it may be held to share with texts, with any 'remainder' being considered unimportant. Material culture does not constitute a text, but in order to understand it there is a necessity to re-present it in textual form. We arrive back at an ambiguity at the heart of material culture studies: the relationship between words and the things, practices, etc. that those words are meant to represent. Material culture studies themselves may be claimed to be an ambiguous art. To write the material world is 'the art of ambiguity'. A linguistic bind thus faces any work that wishes to transcend such a frame of reference. For the child, seeing comes before saying but, in order to communicate that which we see, of necessity we must transform it into words and thus reduce and essentialize our experience of its specificity.

He argued that any study that is involved in studying material culture cannot, in one sense, avoid a doubly 'textual' circuit in which the investigator reads (interprets, looks at, attempts to understand) one text (material substance) to write another. This he took to mean that every archaeologist, anthropologist or art historian is first and foremost a textual critic and all understanding is intertextual – a mediation of one textual form by another. The world is, accordingly, to be conceived as a material medium in which human actions are textually inscribed, written and rewritten through time and history. We live our lives in a material text on which sedimented layers of meaning are both built up and placed side by side. The modern text we live through is like a book which has been printed and reprinted over and over again with words and passages removed, crossed out or written over and others inserted bearing no necessary relationship to the original text: a glass and steel office block next to a sixteenth-century church next to the ruin of a Roman bath.

He has attempted to demonstrate in the book that a textual analogy is one of the most useful positions we have to hand at present in order to understand the significance and meaning of material culture patterning, that the production and use of material culture does share some important common characteristics with texts but equally that material culture diverges from a text in just as many ways. It is this divergence, this difference from a linguistic frame that, he admits, is so difficult to grasp. He claims no satisfactory solution in the book, and has read no work that even begins to articulate an adequate answer. His hope is that by taking linguistic analogies to their limits we may begin to realize their shortcomings and be able to formulate a radically different position. This would perhaps be the truly revolutionary intervention in material culture studies, but it would still have to be written.

In the book he was primarily concerned with three different strands of interpretative theory: semiotics and structuralism, hermeneutics and structural-Marxism. These all come in a large variety of different formulations and what he meant specifically by these labels should be clear in the main body of his text. These perspectives have all been concerned in one way or another with the form and nature of social practices and their relationship to the lived conditions of human existence. In the book he wanted to use these different positions in order to provide diverging perspectives on the relationship between material culture and text. Various strategies are possible: he could either have insisted on holding these perspectives in a relation of irresolvable tension, or simply advocated one of them and denied any validity to the others, or attempted to transcend them all in order to establish a new point of departure. He regarded all the perspectives mentioned above as valuable in different ways and in order to work with them he had to take up the first position and hold them apart in order to establish guidelines for his own interpretative practices. The project of his book, then, was not a totalizing one and as such inevitably involved a position in which contradictions were played up rather than filtered out. Normally, in the reading of a work, the critic will look for contradictions, inevitably locate and emphasize them, rub his or her hands with glee, and proceed to conclude that it is flawed and inadequate. He will do the critic's job for them: his book is a quite miserable failure. It is riddled with contradictions. But he wants to point out that the contradictions have been deliberately built into the text. The result of not bringing out tensions between the different positions he has worked with could, he thinks, only be a work of theoretical ideology, gluing wallpaper over the cracks.

Many books, most particularly those falling into a genre with a general theoretical intent, forging together different perspectives into a new whole and claiming to transcend them all, are wallpapering operations. The 'new' pattern, a pastiche of parts of the old ones, can, of course, be both interesting and stimulating. We need the wallpaper and our lived relation to the world is always to a certain extent an imaginary one. We can never fully be conscious of our conditions of social existence, achieve certain and absolutely coherent knowledge, know precisely why we are acting and thinking as we do. All that we can hope for is to construct models of how to act which will always be defined by absences, a fundamental relation of lack.

In his book it is the cracks in the text that matter as much as the contents lying on either side of them and they are intended for a specific purpose. He does not want to provide the wallpaper but instead open out the possibility for the reader to do it herself or himself – if that is what he or she wants. In other words he does not attempt to provide an overarching theoretical framework which will attempt to pin down the meanings of the rock carvings once and for all. He instead presents different ways of understanding them via semiotic/structuralist, hermeneutic, and structural-Marxist interventions but there is no 'last analysis' in which he evaluates the results of these different positions, 'weighs them up' and decides that one is better than any of the others or that a combination of them would ever give a satisfactory totalizing perspective. Rather, he hoped to show through the example of his theoretical practice, the manner in which different forms of theoretical appropriation take up and emphasize different theoretical objects, inevitably to the exclusion of others. He does not want to give the impression of a total incommensurability and indeed indicates inadequacies in the different interpretative positions presented and the manner in which the various frameworks, perspectives and interpretations could be combined.

The purpose of all this is an attempt to write the past in a different way. Specifically, he made two interventions in this direction. First, the text deviates from those that you are accustomed to read, in that it is 'broken' or partly presented in a non-linear format. He made assumptions and readings which are meant to 'worry' the reader but usually responded to 'worries' that might have arisen at a later stage. In short, he has textually inscribed things later that 'should' have come before, and vice versa. Initially he did not want to write an introduction to his book at all, as it is clearly contradictory to his entire project. In the end he felt it necessary to try and off-set the kinds of criticisms that could be expected from a gross misunderstanding of his enterprise. His final strategy has been a compromise and that is why what was an introduction has become an appendix.

Second, his book is an attempt to write a producer rather than a consumer text. This is why he tries to avoid a linear narrative, sets out to 'worry' the reader and 'fails' to produce an all-embracing and final conclusion as to the meaning of Nämforsen. The levels of meaning in the site are, in effect, being presented like an onion with many different surfaces and no essential, irreducible kernel. Most academic texts that have been written to date are consumer texts. They set up a specific type of relationship between the reader and the writer: the writer produces a text from which, ideally, i.e. from the point of view of the writer, the reader is to be shut out as much as possible. Every possible gap or entry point of the reader should be closed down. The reader is simply to consume the ideas, perhaps to be applied elsewhere, accept the 'coherency' of the argument, and imbibe 'information'. A producer text, by contrast, is one that actively invites the reader to create the text's meaning in relation to its object – in this case the rock carvings at Nämforsen. A producer text is one that actively invites a response: another text. It is a text which attempts to embrace the infinite productivity of discourse itself as a relation between the self and others (see Tilley 1990c for further discussion). A producer text actively seeks to diffuse an authoritarian relationship between the writer and the reader and establish both as dialogic participants, sometimes, of course, as opponents. To use an analogy, what he has been trying to do is to show you not a painting of a prehistoric social landscape with the carvings positioned in it, but more a painting of different ways of painting this landscape which the reader is then to paint. The reader is intended to be a participant and not a spectator, however critical, left at the margins.

Finally, his book attempts to be self-reflexive, to examine its own status and effects. It presents itself as an intervention, a specific set of modalities for understanding, not as a set of disinterested, value-free statements. Although he has worked towards writing a producer text, as he makes clear in the conclusion, this is only a matter of degree. Not anything goes, and he is not free for any and every interpretation but to direct and steer the discussion towards questions such as those to do with power, ideology and meaning that have contemporary implications.

REFERENCES

Ahlén, I. (1975) 'Winter habitats of moose and deer in relation to land use in Scandinavia', *Viltrevy* 9 (3): 45–192.

Althusser, L. (1977) *For Marx*, London: Verso.

Althusser, L. and Balibar, E. (1970) *Reading Capital*, London: New Left Books.

Anderson, A. (1976) 'Prehistoric competition and economic change in northern Sweden', unpublished doctoral dissertation, Cambridge University, U.K.

Anisimov, A. (1963a) 'Cosmological concepts of the people of the north', in H. Michael (ed.) *Studies in Siberian Shamanism*, Toronto: University of Toronto Press.

— (1963b) 'The shaman's tent of the Evenks and the origin of the shamanistic rite', in H. Michael (ed.) *Studies in Siberian Shamanism*, Toronto: University of Toronto Press.

Austin, J. (1962) *How to do Things with Words*, Oxford: Oxford University Press.

Bäckman, L. and Hultkrantz, Å. (1978) *Studies in Lapp Shamanism*, Stockholm: Almqvist and Wiksell.

Bakka, E. (1975) 'Geologically dated rock carvings at Hammer near Steinkjer in Nord-Trondelag', *Arkeologiske Skrifter fra Historisk Museum, Bergen* 2: 7–48.

Barth, F. (1975) *Ritual and Knowledge among the Baktaman of New Guinea*, Oslo: Universitetsforlaget.

Barthes, R. (1973) *Mythologies*, London: Paladin.

— (1984) *Elements of Semiology*, London: Jonathan Cape (reprint in one volume together with *Writing Degree Zero*).

Baudou, E. (1973) 'The cultural concept in the north Swedish stone age', in G. Berg (ed.) *Circumpolar Problems*, Oxford: Pergamon Press.

— (1977) 'Den förhistoriska fångstkulturen i Västernorrland', in E. Baudou and K.-G. Selinge *Västernorrlands Förhistoria*, Motala.

— (1982) 'Den förhistoriska jordbruket i Norrland. Bakgrunden i det arkeologiska fyndmaterialet', in T. Sjövold (ed.) *Introduksjonen av jordbruk i Norden*, Oslo.

Bender, B. (1978) 'Gatherer–hunter to farmer', *World Archaeology* 10: 204–22.

REFERENCES

— (1985) 'Prehistoric developments in the American midwest and in Brittany', in T. Price and J. Brown (eds) *Prehistoric Hunter–Gatherers. The Emergence of Complexity*, Orlando, Florida: Academic Press.

— (1989) 'The roots of inequality', in D. Miller, M. Rowlands and C. Tilley (eds) *Domination and Resistance*, London: Unwin-Hyman.

Berg, G. (1978) 'Zahme Elche in Tradition und Wirklichkeit', *Arv* 34: 5–36.

Bern, J. (1979) 'Ideology and domination: toward a reconstruction of Australian Aboriginal social formation', *Oceania* 50: 118–32.

Berndt, R. (1976) 'Territoriality and the problem of demarcating sociocultural space', in N. Peterson (ed.) *Tribes and Boundaries in Australia*, Canberra: Australian Institute of Aboriginal Studies.

Carpelan, C. (1975) 'Älg-och björnhuvudföremål från Europas nordliga delar', *Finskt Museum*: 5–67.

Christiansson, H. (1961) 'Kring stenåldern i Övre Norrland', *Västerbotten*: 111–85.

Christiansson, H. and Broadbent, N. (1975) 'Prehistoric coastal settlement on the upper Bothnian coast', in W. Fitzhugh (ed.) *Prehistoric Adaptations of the Circumpolar Zone*, The Hague: Mouton.

Clark, J. (1948) 'Objects of southern Scandinavian flint in the northernmost provinces of Norway, Sweden and Finland', *Proceedings of the Prehistoric Society* 14: 219–32.

— (1952) *Prehistoric Europe: The Economic Basis*, Cambridge: Cambridge University Press.

Collier, J. and Rosaldo, M. (1981) 'Politics and gender in simple societies', in S. Ortner and H. Whitehead (eds) *Sexual Meanings*, Cambridge: Cambridge University Press.

Derrida, J. (1976) *Of Grammatology*, Baltimore: John Hopkins University Press.

Douglas, M. (1975) 'Deciphering a meal', in M. Douglas *Implicit Meanings*, London: Routledge & Kegan Paul.

Drake, S. (1918) *Västerbottenlapparna under förre hälften av 1800-talet*, Uppsala.

Düben, G. von (1977) *Om Lappland och Lapparna*, Stockholm: Gidlunds.

Eco, U. (1976) *A Theory of Semiotics*, Indiana University Press, Bloomington.

Edsman C.-M. (1965) 'The hunter, the games and the unseen powers. Lappish and Finnish bear rites', in H. Hvarfner (ed.) *Hunting and Fishing*, Luleå: Norbottens Museum.

Ekman, J. and Iregren, E. (1983) 'Archae-zoological investigations in northern Sweden', *Early Norrland* 8.

Engels, F. (1884) *Origin of the Family, Private Property and the State*, London.

Fjellström, P. (1985) *Samernas samhälle i tradition och nutid*, Stockholm.

Forsberg, L. (1985) 'Site variability and settlement patterns', *Archaeology and Environment* 5, Umeå.

Foucault, M. (1986) 'Of other spaces', *Diacritics* 16: 22–7.

Gadamer, H.-G. (1975) *Truth and Method*, London: Sheed and Ward.

Godelier, M. (1986) *The Making of Great Men*, Cambridge: Cambridge University Press.

REFERENCES

Hagen, A. (1976) *Bergkunst*, Oslo: Cappelens.

Hallström, G. (1938) *Monumental Art of Northern Europe from the Stone Age I. The Norwegian Localities*, Stockholm: Almqvist and Wiksell.

— (1960) *Monumental Art of Northern Sweden from the Stone Age*, Stockholm: Almqvist and Wiksell.

Helskog, K. (1983) 'Helleristningene i Alta. En presentasjon og en analyse av menneskefigurene', *Viking* 47: 5–41.

— (1985) 'Boats and meaning: a study of change and continuity in the Alta fjord, arctic Norway, from 4200 to 500 years BC', *Journal of Anthropological Archaeology* 4: 177–205.

— (1987) 'Selective depictions. A study of 3,500 years of rock carvings from Arctic Norway and their relation to Saami drums', in I. Hodder (ed.) *Archaeology as Long-Term History*, Cambridge: Cambridge University Press.

Hood, B. (1988) 'Sacred rocks: ideological and social space in the north Norwegian stone age', *Norwegian Archaeological Review* vol. 21, no. 2: 65–84.

Huggert, A. (1984) 'Flint also came from the east – a contribution to the knowledge of upper Norrland's prehistory', *Archaeology and Environment* 2: 57–74.

Hultkrantz, Å. (1965) 'Type of religion in the arctic hunting cultures', in H. Hvarfner (ed.) *Hunting and Fishing*, Norbottens: Norbottens Museum.

Hvarfner, H. (ed.) (1965) *Hunting and Fishing*, Norbottens: Norbottens Museum.

Jakobson, R. and Halle, M. (1956) *Fundamentals of Language*, The Hague: Mouton.

Jameson, F. (1981) *The Political Unconscious. Narrative as a Socially Symbolic Act*, London: Methuen.

Janson, S. (1966) 'The land of the hunters', in S. Janson and H. Hvarfner *Ancient Hunters and Settlements in the Mountains of Sweden*, Stockholm: Riksantikvarieämbetet.

Janson, S. and Janson, B. (1980) *Hällristningar vid Nämforsen*, CEWE Press.

Jochelson, W. (1926) *The Yugahir and the Yukaghirized Tungus*, The Jesup North Pacific Expedition Vol. IX (ed. F. Boas), New York: American Museum of Natural History.

Kristiansen, K. (1987) 'Centre and periphery in Bronze Age Scandinavia', in M. Rowlands, M. Larsen and K. Kristiansen (eds) *Centre and Periphery in the Ancient World*, Cambridge: Cambridge University Press.

Layton, R. (1981) *The Anthropology of Art,* London: Elek.

— (1985) 'The cultural context of hunter–gatherer rock art', *Man* 20: 434–53.

— (1989) 'The political use of Australian Aboriginal body painting and its archaeological implications', in I. Hodder (ed.) *The Meanings of Things. Material Culture and Symbolic Expression*, London: Unwin Hyman.

Lévi-Strauss, C. (1962) *Totemism*, London: Merlin.

— (1966) *The Savage Mind*, London: Weidenfeld and Nicolson.

— (1968) 'The concept of primitiveness', in R. Lee and I. deVore (eds) *Man the Hunter*, Chicago: Aldine.

REFERENCES

— (1969) *The Raw and the Cooked*, London: Peregrine Books.

Lewis-Williams, J. (1982) 'The economic and social context of southern San rock art', *Current Anthropology* 23 (4): 429–49.

Lindqvist, C. (1978) 'Älghuvudmotivet i nordeuropeisk plastik och hällkonst', unpublished dissertation, Institute of Archaeology, University of Stockholm.

— (1983) 'Arktiska hällristningsbåtor – spekulationer om kulturellt utbyte via kust – och inlandsvattenvägar i Nordfennoskandia', *Meddelander från Marinarkeologiska Sällskapet* 6: 3–14.

Malmer, M. (1975) 'The rock carvings at Nämforsen, Ångermanland, Sweden as a problem of maritime adaptation and circumpolar relations', in W. Fitzhugh (ed.) *Prehistoric Adaptations of the Circumpolar Zone*, The Hague: Mouton.

— (1981) *A Chorological Study of North European Rock Art*, Stockholm: Almqvist and Wiksell.

Melander, J. (1980) 'Dokumentation och undersökning av hällmålning RAÄ 151 Simsjölandet 1:1, Åsele sn, Västerbotten', unpublished report, Västerbottens Museum.

Michael, H. (ed.) (1963) *Studies in Siberian Shamanism*, Arctic Institute of North America, Toronto: University of Toronto Press (translations from the Russian sources).

Mikkelsen, E. (1986) 'Religion and ecology: motifs and locations of hunters' rock carvings in eastern Norway', in G. Steinslund (ed.) *Words and Objects*, Oslo: Norwegian University Press.

Miller, D. (1987) *Material Culture and Mass Consumption*, Oxford: Blackwell.

Miller, U. and Robertsson, A.-M. (1979) 'Biostratigraphical investigations in the Anundsjö region, Ångermanland, Sweden', *Early Norrland* 12: 1–76.

Moberg, A. (1965) 'Coastal regions and river country in the north and south-west. An archaeologist's list of questions', in H. Hvarfner *Hunting and Fishing*, Norbottens Museum.

Mochi, U. and Carter, T. (1971) *Hoofed Mammals of the World*, London: Trinity Press.

Morgan, L. (1871) *Systems of Consanguinity and Affinity in the Human Family*, London.

— (1877) *Ancient Society*, London.

Munn, N. (1970) 'The transformation of subjects into objects in Walbiri and Pitjantjatjara myth', in R. Berndt (ed.) *Australian Aboriginal Anthropology*, Perth: University of Western Australia Press.

— (1973) *Walbiri Iconography*, Chicago: University of Chicago Press.

Murphy, H. (1989) 'On representing ancestral beings', in H. Murphy (ed.) *Animals into Art*, London: Unwin-Hyman.

Olsen, B. (1984) *Stabilitet og endring. Produksjon og samfunn i varanger 800 f. kr – 1700 e. kr.*, Tromsø: University of Tromsø.

— (1985) 'Arkeologi og etnisitet. Et teoretisk og empirisk bidrag', *Ams-Varia* 15, Stavanger.

— (1990) 'Roland Barthes: from sign to text', in C. Tilley (ed.) *Reading Material Culture*, Oxford: Blackwell.

REFERENCES

Ortner, S. and Whitehead, H. (1981) 'Accounting for sexual meanings', in S. Ortner and H. Whitehead (eds) *Sexual Meanings*, Cambridge: Cambridge University Press.

Pêcheux, M. (1982) *Language, Semantics and Ideology*, London: Macmillan.

Peterson, R. (1955) *North American Moose*, Toronto: University of Toronto Press.

Ramqvist, P., Forsberg, L. and Backe, M. (1985) 'And here was an elk too ... a preliminary report of new petroglyphs at Stornorrforss, Ume river', *Archaeology and Environment* 4: 313–38.

Rheen, S. (1897) 'En kortt relation om Lapparnes lefwarne och sedher wijd skiepellser, samt i många stycken grofwe wildfarellser', *Bidrag til kännedom om de Svenskt folkeliv*, 17, Uppsala.

Ricoeur, P. (1974) *The Conflict of Interpretations: Essays in Hermeneutics*, Evanston: Northwestern University Press.

—— (1981) *Hermeneutics and the Human Sciences*, Cambridge: Cambridge University Press.

Root, D. (1983) 'Information exchange and the spatial configurations of egalitarian societies' in J. Moore and A. Keene (eds) *Archaeological Manners and Theories*, London: Academic Press.

Rowlands, M. (1987) 'Centre and periphery: a review of a concept', in M. Rowlands, M. Larsen and K. Kristiansen (eds) *Centre and Periphery in the Ancient World*, Cambridge: Cambridge University Press.

Saussure, F. de (1966) *Course in General Linguistics*, New York: McGraw-Hill.

Searle, J. (1969) *Speech Acts: An Essay in the Philosophy of Language*, Cambridge: Cambridge University Press.

Simčenko, J. (1978) 'Mother cult among the North-Eurasian peoples', in V. Diószegi and M. Hoppäl (eds) *Shamanism in Siberia*, Budapest: Akadémiai Kiadó.

Simonsen, P. (1986) 'The magic picture: used once or more times?', in G. Steinslund (ed.) *Words and Objects*, Oslo: Norwegian University Press.

Sörensen, S. (1975) 'Livslinje og röntgenperspektiv', *Nicolay* 21: 3–8.

Stanner, W. (1965) 'Religion, totemism and symbolism', in R. Berndt and C. Berndt (eds) *Aboriginal Man in Australia*, Sydney: Angus and Robertson.

Strathern, M. (1980) 'No nature, no culture: the Hagen case', in C. MacCormack and M. Strathern (eds) *Nature, Culture and Gender*, Cambridge: Cambridge University Press.

Strehlow, T. (1970) 'Geography and the totemic landscape in central Australia', in R. Berndt (ed.) *Australian Aboriginal Anthropology*, Perth: University of Western Australia Press.

Sundström, J. (1982) 'Nyfunnen hällmålning', *Jämten* 1: 128.

Tilley, C. (1990a) 'Claude Lévi-Strauss: structuralism and beyond', in C. Tilley (ed.) *Reading Material Culture*, Oxford: Blackwell.

—— (ed.) (1990b) *Reading Material Culture*, Oxford: Blackwell.

—— (1990c) 'On modernity and archaeological discourse', in I. Bapty and T. Yates (eds) *Archaeology after Structuralism*, London: Routledge.

Tillhagen, C.-H. (1985) *Jaktskrock*, Stockholm.

REFERENCES

Tugolukov, V. (1978) 'Some aspects of the beliefs of the Tungus (Evenki and Evens)', in V. Diószegi and M. Hoppál (eds) *Shamanism in Siberia*, Budapest: Akadémiai Kiadó.

Turner, V. (1967) *The Forest of Symbols*, Ithaca: Cornell University Press.

— (1969) *The Ritual Process*, Harmondsworth: Penguin.

Ucko, P. and Rosenfeld, A. (1967) *Palaeolithic Cave Art*, London: Weidenfeld and Nicolson.

Vasilevich, G. (1963) 'Early concepts about the universe among the Evenks (materials)' in H. Michael (ed.) *Studies in Siberian Shamanism*, Toronto: University of Toronto Press.

Vorren, Ø. (1980) 'Samisk bosettning på Nordkalotten, arealdisponering og resursutnytting i historisk-økologisk belysning', in E. Baudou and K.-H. Dahlstedt (eds) *Nord-Skandinaviens historia i Tvärvetenskaplig belysning*, Umeå.

Vorren, Ø. and Manker, E. (1979) *Samekulturen*,Oslo.

Yates, T. (1989) 'Habitus and social space: some suggestions about meaning in the Saami (Lapp) tent ca. 1700–1900', in I. Hodder (ed.) *The Meaning of Things: Material Culture and Symbolic Expression*, London: Unwin Hyman.

INDEX